STUART W. ROSE, PhD.

SUSTAINABILITY

*a personal journey to a built
sustainable community ... and an amazing
picture of what life will soon be like*

ISBN: 1-4392-6383-3
ISBN-13: 9781439263839
Library of Congress Control Number: 2009912254

Acknowledgements

I'm really a synthesizer of many, many ideas from scores of people who have marvelous capabilities and passion for what they do. As you read through this book, I'll cite each of them. One who stands out a bit more than others is John Petersen, a brilliant futurist who is a "walking encyclopedia" of major trends shaping coming times, and who – almost offhandedly – pointed us to sources that have changed our lives in amazing ways.

And when I say "we," none of this book – or the explorations and experiences that led to it – would have happened without Trina Duncan, who – besides being my spouse and partner – is an amazing, insightful, and very gifted being.

Finally, you'll also experience some powerful thoughts, perceptions, and insights from another party, whom I'll simply refer to as "D." Working with Trina and D has made this writing effort – and, in fact, my day-to-day life – a unique and rich experience I could *never* have imagined possible!

Stuart W. Rose, Ph.D.
Autumn, 2009

The Author

Dr. Rose is a registered architect, and a graduate structural engineer. He holds a doctorate in organization development, has been a professor at three major universities, and has worked for several decades as an educator and a consultant to architects, consulting engineers, and other design professionals.

Since the early '90s, he's tracked trends related to our ability to sustain life, as we know it, on our planet. He's initiated a unique pilot project of sustainable housing – homes that do not deplete the earth's resources and that are healthier, more comfortable, and more delightful environments in which to live – testing marketability, to see if truly sustainable homes can compete with traditional housing.

His "Garden Atriums" project has been featured in almost two dozen local, regional, and national papers and magazines, on NPR, and on major regional television programs. He's given presentations at three international sustainability conferences. And, according to one professional society focused on "green" building ...

"You may have the <u>most</u> sustainable homes east of the Mississippi."

Dr. Rose converts concepts about sustainability into concrete sustainable realities.

Table of Contents

The Journey Begins   1

Circa 1985: A Time of Change   3

Circa 1998: A Time of Discontent   11

Circa 1999: A Time to Create   15

Circa 2002: A Time to Sell   31

Circa 2004: The Qu Fü is Born   35

Circa 2007: A Look at Sustainable Living   49

Circa 2008: Going Where Mankind Has Not Gone Before   107

Circa 2009: The Journey to Come   127

The Journey Begins

I am sitting and writing in a home that is quite different from what most homes look like today. I live in a house that has virtually no utility bills, has a tropical garden in its center that oxygenates and purifies air, and is a joy in which to live.

I'd like to share with you how I got here ... along with some ideas about how we can live more enjoyably in our collective futures. I see a future that's *significantly* different than where we are today. Right now, a lot of fear is going around ...

- fear of terrorists;
- fear of economic collapse;
- fear of global climate changes;
- fear of pandemics that could ravage us;
- fear of crime rates and water shortages and ...

I like Franklin Delano Roosevelt's saying,

"The only thing we have to fear is fear itself."

One alternative to fear is: **Hope.**

We're living in a time of great change. Perhaps more change is and will be happening than has happened for thousands of years. And change – especially major change – is unsettling. We all like to depend on certain things ...

- a favorite food;
- a dentist we've seen for years;
- (for women) a stylist that "knows my hair";
- a vacation spot we've relished since we were small children;
- Or a government that – despite flaws – we can count on for some things.

I recall a line from the film, *Memphis Belle,* in which one of the crew asked another which design he liked best for a hamburger chain he was planning to open after the war. His colleague questioned why people would want to see the same design and eat same food – everywhere they went. His response ...

"It's comforting."

And when change occurs, and people, places, and institutions on which we've depended for years are all changing, it's uncomfortable ... disconcerting. It's the "fear of the unknown." And many "gloom and doom" messages grow out of that.

The purpose of this book is to share a picture with you of what has a high potential of occurring ... and soon. And what's even more important, what's in store for us – despite the inevitable trauma of transition – will be ...

FANTASTIC!

This is more than wishful thinking.

I want to share with you a picture of what I believe has been happening in our world, so you understand the transformation that's happening and feel less fearful. And I'd like to paint a picture of where I believe we're heading. Some aspects are really clear for me, and others are still a bit fuzzy. But I can honestly tell you ... despite the discomfort that change will bring ... I can't wait to get there!

So, the goal of this book is to share that vision with you. However, many people whom I respect – including one professional author who's written several best-sellers – advise me to relate everything to you as a personal story that provides a thread from where I began to where I am now. By sharing the journey I have taken – and am continuing to take – you may be able to bypass some of the obstacles I've experienced, and enjoy the positive outcomes more fully and more easily.

Writing in the first person is somewhat uncomfortable for me. I go out and try to do positive things each day, and earn a living and enjoy a good life ... which I think we all try to do. But I seem to have some qualities that enable me to "go off the deep end" and venture where I never thought I'd venture. So ...

Circa 1985: A Time of Change

For years, I've worked as a consultant to the "design professions" – architects, consulting engineers, landscape architects, interior designers, and environmental scientists – all of whom, in different ways, are stewards of our built and natural environment. My own background began with degrees in architecture and in structural engineering, and then a master's degree focused on urban design ... why some neighborhoods or business districts feel better than others. I am also a registered architect, which affects my perspective of the world.

Actually, the term, "consulting," is too broad. What I've done – and still do – is teach short courses to these professionals. In school, people get technical training – in design or in engineering. When they enter into a professional services firm, they begin by applying what they've learned in college – with supervision, and with many "real world" constraints, such as budgets and schedules and other client issues they need to address. If they do well, after a few years, they're then told ...

> *"We'd now like you to also contribute to our firm's marketing, and help us bring in new clients – as well as maximize our repeat business."*

And for many professionals, that's uncomfortable. In fact, one person once said ...

> *"My engineers would sooner have a root canal than make a cold call."*

While many methods exist for getting to know new clients – other than the "cold call" – most of these professionals have never had training in bringing in clients or projects. When any of us is asked to do something for which we've had no training, discomfort usually follows. Plus, marketing is a more "humanistic" domain, as opposed to the applied physical science orientation of their professions.

Many moons ago, a behavioral science colleague – who is in the field in which I happened to earn my doctorate – and I developed a system by which these technically trained professionals could more comfortably relate to their clients. The system, known as "the Mandeville Techniques," enables professionals to:

- Comfortably meet new clients;
- Comfortably cultivate professional-client trust relationships;
- Make more responsive proposals and presentations to their clients;
- And – perhaps most important – ensure high levels of client satisfaction, so they can sustain a long-term relationship with that client.

And so, I've traveled across the country – and occasionally out of the country – to conduct these one-, two-, and three-day hands-on training programs. The professionals felt helped and were able to contribute significantly to their firms' success. I enjoyed both professional satisfaction and a comfortable livelihood. Then ...

The 1980s came along.

Work that had been plentiful suddenly disappeared. Entire markets – such as office buildings or schools or highways or municipal water treatment, etc. – shifted. Some shrank. Some grew. Some were unaffected and continued steadily. The problem was:

> If a firm specialized in designing schools – or highways or hospitals or airports, etc. – and if the amount of work in those markets diminished, then the professional firms serving those markets would be hurt. Profits diminish. Some staff are laid off. And morale suffers.

We – and here I introduce my consulting partner and spouse, Trina Duncan - began to help our clients identify markets that were growing. In that process ...

- I begin by conducting a focus group of "clients and knowledgeable third parties," to brainstorm what they see as markets that are likely to grow over the coming five to ten years. Then ...

- Trina conducts market research on what seems the hottest markets. First, a colleague with a library science degree culls a load of solid information for each market. Then Trina phone-interviews clients in that market, to see what they see happening in their market in the coming years – and to learn what help they'd like from clients such as ours. (Trina actually *likes* cold calling; better her than me!)

- After a series of interviews, a pattern usually emerges ... a picture of what will be happening in that market and why. (These projections have been amazingly accurate.)

- The process concludes with a "strategic planning retreat" in which (1) market information is shared; (2) clients select the markets they most desire; and (3) we help clients develop a set of actions for getting into those markets, to ensure them of a more successful future.

Now, why is all this relevant to "sustainability"?

To get a sense of shifts in markets, we began reading "trends literature" on a regular basis. The daily news – in newspapers, or on radio or TV – tends to focus on events. Trends literature looks at series of events that form trends. They show the 27 dots and the likely direction for the next dots. With this reading, we moved from "daily events" and a state of childlike innocence – in which we saw the world through small, unrelated events – to an understanding that so many events are connected and form a "big picture." We began seeing the world differently.

Then, in 1985, came ...

Megatrends, the best-seller by John Naisbitt. It came out in the midst of the turbulence in our marketplace, and forecast (quite accurately) ten major and specific directions that were coming.

Do you remember the system he used to identify those trends?

Naisbitt used a system that he attributed to the OSS, used for spying on Japan and Germany during World War II. We'd read newspapers from those countries, and sort the articles by topic. Then we'd count the column inches of articles, by topic, and measure changes in the number of column inches, over time.

> Germany's articles showed increasing concern for energy conservation, which implied fuel shortages, so we focused our bombing raids on destroying their petroleum processing facilities.

> Japan's articles indicated concern for food, encouraging people to have home gardens to grow more food themselves. We focused our war efforts on sinking their cargo ships.

Naisbitt identified five states he called "bellwether" states – places where all changes in the United States have begun. He read their papers and measured column inches, by topic, over time. And from that effort he was able to accurately identify major trends that would be affecting all of us. If a business were in line with any of his projected growth trends, it would usually do well.

Megatrends was probably the first book of its kind to become a major best seller, and to raise our level of consciousness about major trends, and the potential for shifts in entire marketplaces. And it led Trina and me to begin reading multiple sources – books and periodicals – that provided trends information, so we could be more responsive to our clients ... and also so we could simply be more aware, personally, of the "big picture" of what was really going on in our world.

One source that's had a huge impact on us has been WorldWatch Institute, led, at the time, by Lester Brown. WorldWatch provided global statistical information about all sorts of trends happening in our world that affect us all. For instance ...

> I recall a flow of data concerning depletion of our fisheries. Orange Roughy, for instance, was caught at a slightly deeper level in the ocean, off of New Zealand. It was fished out in 14 years. It was a tasty white-meat fish that was popular – and has since disappeared. Major large ocean fish – including tuna and swordfish – are now 90% fished out.

Beyond heating, cooling, electricity, water, and air quality ... food is a growing sustainability issue. The good news, from Steve Jones of Mount Shasta, California ...

"Currently, there is enough food grown on the planet to provide every single man, woman, and child with approximately 3500 calories of nutrition per day. (A normal healthy diet takes in between 2000 and 2500 calories per day.)"

The bad news, from multiple sources ...

Between 18 million and 40 million people (statistics vary) now die every year of starvation. Six million are children. In fact, malnutrition is a growing problem even in the United States.

Global warming causes "desertification." Yearly, arable land the size of Rhode Island is no longer available to feed growing populations.

From Dr. Ransom Myers and Dr. Boris Worm, *"Only 10% of all large fish are left in global oceans. Ninety percent of all large fish, including tuna, marlin, swordfish, sharks, cod. and halibut. are <u>gone</u>."*

The question to ask, then, is ...

What will be the impact on our food supply?

- More fish farms?
- Shifts in diet away from fish?
- Or even ... potential mass food shortages?

Once you begin reading trends literature, your thinking shifts a bit. You tend to look at most articles as a potential piece of a trend. Another example ...

"Evidence from prehistoric times indicates an oxygen content of the atmosphere well above today's 21 percent of total volume. Oxygen ... has decreased in recent times ... The oxygen content of the atmosphere now dips to 19 percent over impacted areas and is down to 12 to 17 percent over major cities. This level is insufficient to keep body cells, organs, and the immune system functioning at full efficiency; cancers and other degenerative diseases are likely to develop."

Dr. Ervin Laszlo

The quality of air – forgetting about smog, and just thinking about oxygen – that we need to sustain healthy lives is actually diminishing, and because you see nothing in the media about it, nothing is likely being done to correct this problem.

Around 1956, Dr. M. King Hubbert, a geologist, had been studying the behavior of oil wells. He found that once discovered, they could expect a regular increase in barrels-per-day production ... for a time. As nothing keeps going up forever, a well would hit a peak – a maximum amount of oil that could be extracted in a day. That production level would stay relatively constant ... a plateau ... for a while. Then ...

As the well began to be depleted, the amount per day would taper off.

Then he wondered what the behavior of an entire field of wells looked like … and he found the same production profile. As one well began to drop off, a new one would be discovered. But the entire oil field also had a "peak" amount, then a plateau, and an eventual decline.

Next, Dr. Hubbert looked at multiple oil fields – for the entire United States. The same profile seemed to hold true. In 1956 he projected that the United States would reach Peak Oil – the point at which daily U.S. oil production was at its maximum – in 1970. He and his projections were held in disregard, until …

1972.

By then, production amounts showed that Dr. Hubbert's projections were accurate. From that point, we became dependent on imported oil … and on the Middle East.

He also projected that we'd reach "Global Peak Oil" in 1996. With the gas shortage scares around 1980 and with increasing concerns about oil price escalation, consumption trailed off somewhat. The Saudis – and the world – reached Global Peak Oil in 2006-2007, which was about ten years later than Dr. Hubbert's projections.

What are the implications?

While the price per barrel will have daily or seasonal fluctuations, as demand continues to grow and supply has passed its maximum, reserves will be depleted and prices will escalate. Not "might be" … will be. Our use of oil will change as its cost escalates. Demand will curtail, until a balance is reached. At, say, $10/gallon …

- Gas cars will likely become rare and much more efficient.
- All-electric cars will become more commonplace.
- Natural gas power plants will diminish.
- Homes will use oil alternatives.

But a key piece of machinery needing a pint of an expensive oil-based lubricant will still have it. I've recently noticed an increasing number of articles about:

- Increases in wind machine efficiency and wind farms – with some European countries generating a high percent of their power that way and with new installations in the Midwestern states of the U.S.;

- Increases in the efficiency of photovoltaic panels, and the growth of PV panels on individual buildings and, out West, of whole PV farms;

- Increases in the efficiency of batteries – the amount of power they store, their weight, their cost, their longevity, etc. So …

Regardless of what multinational corporations and the governments they influence would like to see, you can be assured of seeing a rapidly growing percent of U.S., power coming from these two renewable energy sources. You can rest assured that all-electric cars – scheduled to hit our market in 2010 – will do well initially and will enjoy regular growth in sales.

Seeing a recent article about a new battery that's the size of a refrigerator and can store enough power for an entire home, we may see new housing developments that are totally off-grid, providing greater reliability with *no* utility bill.

And one last trend illustration – which may be our biggest coming challenge ...

In 1997, I recall seeing a small announcement at the bottom of the front page of the *Washington Post.* It simply said that the People's Republic of China just announced that this was the first year in its history in which it would be a net food importer. The announcement had no in-depth follow-up article. However ...

WorldWatch's *"State of the World"* had a more insightful article about China's food problems. It cited a 25-year straight-line decline in food production that simply had crossed from a diminishing amount of exports to the beginning of net imports.

And how would that affect us, in the United States?

Because of China's size, if that straight line were to continue, at some point the rest of the world would not have sufficient surplus – at any price – to sell it. The best-case scenario said that point would be 2016 ... and that's *best* case.

In the early '90s, another term began to surface, with increasing regularity ...

"Sustainability."

Initially, I thought the environmental groups were searching for a new term to maintain public interest in their causes. We could only read about Spotted Owls so long before it was no longer newsworthy. However, as I saw the detail of the statistics, I realized they were talking about ...

Our ability to sustain life on Planet Earth!

And the number of column inches focused on "sustainability" was steadily growing, which raises the question ...

How can you burn out an entire planet?

While we began reading about trends to help our clients reposition their firms towards growth markets, trends such as China's food production, depletion of the world's fisheries, Global Peak Oil, and the emergence of genuine concerns about our ability to sustain increasingly commanded my personal attention. Also ...

The late '80s and the '90s were busy times for us. An increasing number of professional firms – both new clients and repeat clients – kept me hopping. While the professional satisfaction was good and the income flow was good, I fatigued.

Even though the repetitive lecture elements were on video and seen in advance, even the training aspects – observing participant breakthroughs or difficulties, and watching people evolve their skill levels – began to feel repetitive. Plus ...

Two to four days away ... on planes ... in hotels ... every week ... is tiring.

And I began wondering ...

"How many Mandeville workshops are enough?"

Trina and I had long discussions about what to do. We know that once someone's enthusiasm for what he's doing wanes, he needs to make a change. But when you have your own small consulting practice, you can't just stop.

We all need to be productive and also make a living. So ...

Off to a career counselor!

Circa 1998: A Time of Discontent

I found a career consulting organization, The Rockport Institute, in a nearby suburban area. As I assume many of these professionals do, he ran a battery of tests:

- personal traits,
- work & leisure preferences,
- and ... a search for some useful skills.

With a doctorate in applied behavioral sciences, I'm familiar with many such tests – and use several with clients. The biggest discovery they made was that a side of me that has design skills – creating physical things – was not being used at all in the kind of consulting and training work I was doing. And after all the testing and all the sifting of possibilities, the top "drivers" that surfaced were:

1. **Making the world a better place.** From ages 8 to 20 I spent a lot of time canoe tripping in Canada. One of the creeds I was taught was:

    "Always leave the campsite better than it was when you got there – even though you have no idea if it will ever be used again."

    If you've done any tripping you were probably taught the same. It also seems a reasonable way of approaching how we live all the time.

2. **Creativity.** I have a difficult time thinking about "being creative" for the sake of inventing something new. But if I see a way of doing something that simply makes sense, I really don't care whether or not others are doing it. It just seems like "the right way to do it."

3. **Problem solver.** That *is* me! One of my mentors likened me to a *Star Trek* episode in which a "pet robot" was programmed to destroy anything that wasn't perfect. I do have a difficult time just accepting things that clearly could be better ... when I'm sure they could be improved. (It drives people who are close to me crazy at times.)

4. **Driven.** As an architect and a structural engineer, I like projects. I actually need them. They present a problem and almost beg me to solve them. And when I do come up with a great solution to some problem, I really sleep well that night. However, I'm also finding that problems, for me, now need to have some "higher purpose." Then I have the passion that's needed to address them.

Three guidelines evolved from these tests and the traits they surfaced ... which have affected my life since then ...

1. Global issues are coming to a head. We need better ways for creating
    a better quality of life environment that supports life sustainably.

2. There's always a new frontier of possibilities; my job is to break through
    and discover them.

3. Sitting idle is, for me, useless; my job is to keep moving, at all costs.

A brief comment about that second trait ... breaking through new frontiers. My doctoral work was in what's known as "organization development" ... the people side of
an organization. Why some companies are effective and others are not. Upon arrival
on campus for my doctoral work, the mantra that was laid on me was:

> *"You're being trained to be an organizational change agent. You should
> be able to enter into an organization, quickly see the problems, and
> cause changes to occur that make the organization more effective."*

What I learned is, even though there may be a better way, people will fight you – and
not very subtly or politely – even when you try to cause positive change. I remember
stories from the 1960s, when electric typewriters were being introduced. Typists
would find all sorts of reasons not to use them, and would fight people trying to help
them learn to use them. They may thank you later ... but *much* later!

We are all creatures of habit. It's not some "out there" concept. Each of us has ways
of doing things we find comfortable and effective. We may get praise for what we do.
And we may be paid well for what we do. And – theoretically – there's always a better
way. But, when you get down to it, we usually like how we do things.

And when someone comes along and tells us there's a better way ... look out.

What the organization development faculty never taught us – and this was a doctoral
course, so it was kind of "the end of the line, with no sequel" – was ...

> *"When you try to cause change, even with the noblest of intentions,
> be prepared for a <u>lot</u> of pain to come your way!"*

It may be an odd trait of mine, but I have no problem being on the receiving side of
pain ... if the change I'm trying to cause seems worthwhile. I'll take risks that I view
as very sane, which very successful friends tell me are nuts. For example ...

> A very successful developer friend was all over my case – vehemently
> so – because of an unproven venture I was planning. Paraphrasing,

> *"Wait until you see the bell curve established and going up.
> That's when your risk is lower and your profits are higher."*

And from a business perspective, he's absolutely right. But ...

Someone has to begin any new trend, even though I know many such attempts often fail miserably. I find that if the reason seems worthwhile, I'll readily take the risk and even receive the pain that invariably surfaces when we try to do something in a different way. I also recall the saying ...

> *"Ya pays yer nickel and ya takes yer chances."*

Somehow, I've always had an ability to enter into situations – a new course, a trip to Tibet, the "Iron Rooster" (the trans-Siberian train), or the North Pole in the dead of winter – and sense that I'll somehow survive and come out, intact, at the other end ... and often for the better, even though there's no proof of that.

Putting all the pieces together ...

> I needed to diversify my career.

> I had growing concerns about sustainability.

> I'm a problem solver who needs to work with design elements.

> And I seem to have no problem whatever in venturing into the unknown.

Many issues in the world we all read about, but so many of the issues are so huge and so broad that, as a single individual, I don't believe I can affect them. But when it came to our ability to sustain on planet Earth, I thought ...

> *"Everyone needs a house.*

> *"Let's create a house that's totally sustainable, so that if we build a million of them, we wouldn't deplete the earth's resources.*

> *"And let's see how well such a house can compete with traditional housing, otherwise it will never be replicated and become mainstream, and we'll never reach the numbers needed to make a real difference."*

The premise sounded simple enough.

The next step, then, was to create a design concept for a "sustainable home" ...

Circa 1999: A Time to Create

In 1979 and 1980, when one of the oil crises was happening, the Department of Energy gave a grant to the American Institute of Architects Research Corporation, to teach architects and mechanical engineers how to do passive solar design. The Research Corporation then phoned me and asked if I could work with four of the top passive solar experts in the United States, get them to share formulas and methods, and help them create a hands-on training program that they could teach.

One of their experts was from western Wisconsin, where it's mostly cold and dry. One was from Princeton, New Jersey, where it's primarily cold and humid. One was from Houston, Texas, where is mostly warm and humid. And the fourth was from Phoenix, Arizona, where it's largely hot and dry. In those four climatic regions, the issues are clearly different, and the tactics for creating comfortable living environments in a "passive solar" way are also quite different.

As a facilitator of this workshop, known as "The Passive Studio," I had to attend each session. While I certainly didn't function in any instructional way, other than helping the four experts with different "instructional methods," I slowly began – by repetitive exposure – to understand what passive solar design was all about …

> "Passive solar" means that the building itself is the collector.
> (Panels added to the roof are "active solar" collectors.)
>
> Heating and cooling and lighting could maximize the
> use of the sun to create comfort with minimal utility bills.

By the end of the two-day workshop, every architect and mechanical engineer could create a design – and most brought actual projects with them, so they'd apply their new learning to real world situations – that was 100% passive solar. Not "efficient" or "green," but a measurable 100% passive solar heated.

I also learned that passive solar design did not have to increase the cost of a building one-nickel. For example, if you decrease north-facing windows and increase south-facing windows, you increase incoming solar heat – "insolation" – and can generate what you need to be totally comfortable. If you increase insulation, which does cost more, you can decrease the size of your furnace and ductwork.

In passive solar design, the most efficient shape is a sphere. It has the least skin area for the volume. Our intestines are just the opposite – long and squiggly with a lot of surface – maximum surface for the volume – because their role is to absorb. Retail strip centers, with front walls of glass, are about as inefficient as possible.

In general, spheres aren't a practical form to construct or in which to live. But …

How about a cube?

Make the house a "hollow square." Let the rooms surround a central courtyard – an atrium – as was done in the Indus Civilization, by the Greeks and Romans, and has since been done in many temperate regions of the world. In the Southern regions of the United States, you might see a hollow square design, with sliding glass doors looking into a central garden – often with fine netting overhead, to keep birds and mosquitoes out.

Atrium homes are urban dwellings. They're introverted, in that everything looks inward, and provides great privacy. I might not use the concept on a mountain-top site, in which I wanted to enjoy commanding views. But – most of us live in urban settings, and privacy can be quite valuable. Then I thought ...

Unlike what's been done previously, why not put a large skylight over that atrium?

Now the central courtyard becomes an interior space, and what the passive solar designers call a "heat sink." The sun comes in by day. The sun's heat is absorbed by the thermal mass of the flooring – such as brick, stone, concrete, or porcelain tiles. If a desired winter temperature is 68°F, by 3:00 p.m. the atrium may warm to approximately 72°F. After the sun goes down, the flooring radiates its warmth back into the home. By 7:00 the next morning, the atrium temperature may fall to 64°F. Then the sun rises and the cycle repeats itself.

The exterior walls and roof – and even under the floor – are also heavily insulated, (R-30 to R-75,) so that the solar heat that comes in, stays in. (An R-Value indicates *insulation's* resistance to heat flow. The higher the *R-value*, the greater the *insulation's* effectiveness. Traditional homes may have R-values in the mid-teens.)

Just as the ocean never gets hot or cold, in passive solar design you'll have gentle rises above and gentle declines below your desired temperature. It's actually very comfortable, and has no "forced hot air" periodically blowing on you.

That's the concept that somehow made sense to me. So ...

Away I went to bounce the idea off of some experts!

First, I shared the idea with Rodney Wright, one of the four instructors of The Passive Studio. Rodney and his wife, Syd, seem like the original "earth parents." For years, he automatically designed every building to heat itself – as automatically as every architect works to ensure that your roof won't leak. They live in lovely, but minimal homes. They compost their organic waste. They do hydroponic gardening and enjoy their chemical-free foods. They're practical. And they still go to every course they can that might add another positive twist to environments they create.

They also designed an all-solar town in western Wisconsin, where the winters are actually more severe than those in nearby Minneapolis. Rodney and Syd gave me a very positive reaction to the atrium concept. That was from a passive solar design perspective. The other issue, however, is ...

Marketability.

If we create a magnificent sustainable home that can't compete in the marketplace with traditional housing ... we would have just created a one-of-a-kind anomaly and would never be able to achieve the numbers needed to make a real difference.

So ... off to see someone who's relatively expert in real estate.

A colleague in Atlanta, Dr. Carl Tschappat, taught a workshop for architects and engineers on how to develop their own projects. He was also head of the Real Estate Department at Georgia State University and has been a partner in a long-established real estate appraisal firm. He might have a sense of whether such a different concept would sell.

When I arrived, in late afternoon, he wanted to see what I'd been cooking up. And when I shared my thoughts and some sketches with him ... it set him back. It just was not – for better or worse – what was "being done." And going against an established trend meant higher risk and lower probability of success. In the morning, Dr. Tschappat seemed to have mused over the concept during the night ...

> *"Your atrium and garden are thirty-five feet deep; that's deeper than my entire house! It's not a little postage stamp. And looking into this kind of a garden could be quite appealing. But, let me show you what's selling."*

And we got into his car and visited a few current developments that were supposedly "hot." These were what are now referred to as "McMansions," large homes with (often) odd circulation patterns, that were not all that far apart, and that were likely to have large heating and cooling bills. Dr. Tschappat, with his dry humor, scoffed at these homes, as they didn't really make a lot of sense from a "practical living" point of view. Then he said ...

> *"While they really make no sense, this is what's selling."*

Dr. Tschappat's recommendation for me was to find an experienced and successful developer – someone who knows his market and knows how to sell new homes – and ask that person to coach me. He cautioned that while the "product" I was envisioning actually made a lot of sense, it would be a lot more difficult asking people to buy one, because it was not mainstream. A home is usually our biggest purchase. We don't want to look like we've made a stupid decision. And — if it's a new concept, how do we know we'll be able to re-sell our home at some future time?

Between the financial commitment we were about to make – as in "all our personal assets" – and because of the challenges Dr. Tschappat posed, marketing loomed as the biggest challenge we'd be facing.

And the search for a coach began ...

I was living in Washington, D.C., at the time. From the staff at the National Association of Homebuilders, I secured the names of 25 successful homebuilders in the metropolitan D.C. area – most in suburban Maryland or Virginia – who were also reputed to be more innovative and more open to new ideas. I phoned every one of those people, briefly sharing my intent and my desire to have a successful developer provide me with guidance as I attempted to make the vision a reality.

Not one would even meet with me. Paraphrasing their comments ...

> *"If you want to build houses, look in the magazines, see what's selling,
> and copy what they're doing. Stay in the mainstream or go bankrupt."*

Technically, that's true ... from a marketing perspective. If everyone – for whatever reason – is buying 3,000-square-foot, red brick, ranch-style homes, and if you build some like that, you're in tune with the current market sentiment, and should be able to sell the homes you've built. But – from a sustainability perspective – we're living "on borrowed time," and I knew the bubble would burst at some point.

Finally, I found a successful developer in southeast Virginia, who said ...

> *"Bring down your plans and ideas; I'll pull some of my people together
> and we'll give you our honest reactions and suggestions."*

I remember sharing all my thinking and the concept drawings I'd done, and the head of the developer's marketing department asked,

> *"Who is your target market?"*

My response was ...

> *"Whoever would like to buy one."*

And he said ...

> *"That's <u>not</u> how you sell real estate!"*

I knew – especially because I work as a marketing consultant – that he was right. Yet, I had no clue about how to identify and focus in on some target market group for the purpose of real estate sales. And I also knew that I really needed these people to coach me – or I might go bankrupt. I still recall the comment made by the developer, Buddy Spencer, as we left that first meeting ...

> *"You know, you're kind of a pioneer. And pioneers are people with arrows in their backs! If I give you advice, and if – despite all our best efforts – your houses don't sell, I don't want you to hate me."*

From that meeting, four major activities ensued ...

1. **Market research.** We needed to know if our vision was a pipe dream best left on the shelf, or if potential buyers – people in the same financial bracket – might favor the idea.

2. **Funding.** We needed money to buy a site, to pay design fees, and to build a model home we could show, to entice others to do likewise.

3. **A site.** The saying in real estate is, "Location, location, location." Where would the ideal site be for creating so unique a development?

4. **Drawings.** It was time to sit down with Rodney Wright – and other consultants – and pore through all sorts of details, so that we could convert the overall concept into a constructible physical reality.

Beginning with market research, Buddy suggested that Trina and I hire a consultant who regularly conducts focus groups. To prepare to share the concepts, we also had computer graphic drawings done of the design concept, along with a brief animation video that showed how the project would actually look.

We conducted two focus groups, with twelve people per group. We explained our goals, shared the drawings with them, and showed them the video. Then, we did a lot of listening. No one was against the environmental aspects. They especially liked that the homes would be single story, as people seem to get hip and knee problems by the time they turn 45 or 50. And they stressed factors such as storage, storage, and more storage. And ... they wanted to keep maintenance minimal.

As Trina and I drove back to Washington after the focus groups, I remember asking our consultant, without looking through her notes, what she thought, overall ...

> *"Do it. I've never conducted focus groups that were so positive about a new concept. I'll summarize details in a report, but ... <u>do</u> it."*

As nothing happens without the money to make it happen, that was our second order of business. And that provided quite an education.

Every business has a style. And when we work with people in that business, we need to be comfortable with their style. Bankers have a particular style. But I've somehow never been very compatible with their style. Trina is much better with lenders, so she usually takes the lead here. And even though we had just finished our most profitable year ever – so that our financial statement looked very good, and we had many years of a successful practice, and an excellent credit rating – the bankers with whom I spoke all (politely) rejected me.

> *"It's not your financial statement or personal credibility; we just can't finance something like what you're proposing."*

Here's the problem ...

When you buy a house and apply for a mortgage, the lender needs to have an appraisal done. If, for whatever reason, you're unable to repay your mortgage, and if the lender needs to repossess your home, the lender needs to know – with some certainly – how much can be reasonably expected when your home is sold.

Appraisers typically seek out five or so homes that are as similar to yours as possible, that are as near to yours as possible, and that sold as recently as possible. Then they examine these "comparables," compare them to the home you're buying, and report to the lender what they perceive is the value of your home … the price the lender could reasonably expect to receive for your home within, say, 90 days.

The system is reasonable.

Were I a lender, I'd likely want the same assurances.

But the system inhibits innovation. Homebuilders think of innovation as, perhaps, building bookshelves next to a fireplace … or having a breakfast nook with banquette seating and decorative windows. They think in terms of minor features that may be appealing to buyers, but enable the house to seem normal – "comparable."

Then we had a breakthrough …

Trina phoned the Bank of America, with whom we had the mortgage on our home. She set up a meeting with one of their loan officers. We had paid down ten years of our mortgage, had no late payments, and had a home that was appreciating rapidly … as in-close, historic Georgetown homes often do. Trina told her what we were planning, shared financial statements with her, and asked the loan officer what the best way might be for us to secure the funding we needed for our project.

A few weeks later, I happened to receive the call from the loan officer …

> *"We've just approved you for a line of credit of up to $667,000, using your Georgetown home as collateral."*

I thought I'd be elated. It actually frightened me.

It's one thing to play with ideas and even to spend a few dollars on travel or on professional fees, to explore an idea. It's something else to make a commitment that empties your pockets.

We also knew we'd have to cash in stocks we'd purchased – essentially liquidating all our assets in order to be able to make this sustainable housing vision a reality.

And what shocked me the most …

When I told Trina – who manages our money and is generally conservative about money – that we were approved by Bank of America, she said, without hesitation …

"Do it."

No negotiation.

No "what if" conversations.

And no discussion of "pros and cons."

Instead of elation, this hit me like a sledgehammer. It was "fish or cut bait" time. As a friend of mine puts it, *"Money talks; bullshit walks!"* We've all come to times when we played with some idea or another – often for years. And when that idea suddenly gets to a point at which we need to make a serious personal commitment, we're often challenged to see just how serious we really were with our idea.

Instead of euphoria, a heavy sense of responsibility settled over me.

We were about to go into a very deep hole – the greatest debt we'd ever had – to see if an idea I thought had merit would play out in the marketplace and would then help contribute to a solution in the issue of sustainability. But ...

As I mentioned earlier, I've always had the capacity to somehow venture into situations that seemed worthwhile – even situations that struck many bright people as strange – and believe I'd somehow survive ... and maybe do something positive. Securing funding was the first step in making this vision a reality. And it then paved the way for the third step, finding a site ...

Buddy showed me around Hampton Roads' peninsula, thinking about where the best site might be. ("Hampton Roads" was a British name, as they used the York and James rivers as roads for their ships. The peninsula includes Newport News, Hampton, Williamsburg, Jamestown, Yorktown, Poquoson, and a few other communities. Hampton Roads' "south side" includes Norfolk, Virginia Beach, etc.)

After some reflection, Buddy had two recommendations ...

1. *"Build your project in Poquoson. It has the highest per capita income in all of Hampton Roads. NASA and Langley Air Force Base are only three miles away. Jefferson Labs is about five miles away. And technical people may be more willing to forego "Williamsburg Colonial charm" for modern technology. And – Poquoson has one of the top school systems in the state – which is critical in real estate sales.*

2. *"Find a small lot and just build a small cluster of homes. You don't need to build thirty or fifty or more homes to see whether your concept is marketable. A smaller site, for a small cluster of homes is more in line with your small financial resources and inexperience."*

I'd never heard of Poquoson (Pa-Koh'-Sun). In my wildest thoughts ...

I'd never thought of moving from a very walkable and historic Georgetown high-density urban community to this little town of 11,000 at the bottom of Chesapeake Bay. But if someone who seems to know what he's doing – and who's made a lot of money doing it, for many years – says this is the place to be … it's the place to be.

The idea of creating a small cluster of homes seemed reasonable. We wouldn't have the same social sense as a community might that had fifty homes, but it was more of a bite-sized effort. I recall showing my developer coach my financial statement, as I was preparing to meet with a local banker. I was glowing, as we'd just finished our best year ever. He looked at the numbers and said …

"Well, you're not playing with very deep pockets, are you?"

That off-hand statement – not intending in any way to be hurtful – really opened my eyes. When you have a small business, you add up what you need every month – salary and overhead expenses. And you look at your projected revenue, to be sure you can pay all your expenses – and maybe have a little left over, *"in case."* In development, you go into a very deep indebtedness hole – as you buy land and build structures – and come out of that hole when you sell those structures … several months or even years later. The rhythm is very different, as are the numbers.

Working with one of the developer's Realtors, we found a little 5.1-acre site that was a small abandoned farm, fronting on the main road that went through the commercial section of Poquoson. The developer was pleased, because …

"You need a site that has a <u>lot</u> of visibility, not something tucked away in the woods. Your concept is unusual. People need to see it – lots of people need to see it. Almost everyone in town will be going past your homes. You need that kind of visibility for what you're trying.

"And the acreage only will allow you to build seven homes. But that's enough to see whether there's a market for your ideas. If they sell like hot-cakes, you can always find a larger site the next time out."

Shortly thereafter, we became the proud owners of a heavily trafficked site in a town I never knew existed. But somehow it all made sense. The developer seemed to know – without hesitation – what he was doing. That made me feel comfortable both about Dr. Tschappat's suggestion that I get a coach, and that this particular developer had agreed to coach me and thought of things I simply didn't consider.

With a site in hand, I was ready for the fourth step, the drawings.

Rodney Wright reminds me of a very personable Irish gnome – the kind you see marching in parades on St. Patrick's Day. He's short, has wonderful wavy white hair, a small potbelly, a great laugh, and loves to spin yarns and tell jokes. But … Rodney's also very practical and very committed to designing buildings that take care of themselves with what comes to the site – especially the sun. After many dialogues and visits …

We had a set of construction drawings for our first Garden Atrium home.

And there's more ...

Rodney focused on heating and cooling and daylighting. He was also sensitive to air quality – specifying materials that did not off-gas. Specifically...

- Sherwin-Williams and Benjamin Moore had just introduced zero VOC (for volatile organic compounds) paint. I discovered that paint actually off-gasses for ten years. And when people repaint after six or seven years, the process begins again.

- Plywood and melamine also off-gas, so all kitchen and bath cabinetry was specified to be solid wood.

- Dyes in fabrics – clothing or upholstery or carpeting – are set with formaldehyde. He specified dye-free wool carpeting with a natural hemp backing.

That way, we eliminated the three biggest causes of off-gassing in a home – and the allergy symptoms, rashes, and headaches that accompany them. Most homes, it turns out, are a lot "sicker" than we think. And we usually think the problem is ...

Us.

What actually happens is, our body's natural immune system gets worn down, protecting us from the airborne toxins. That's what leads to rashes or headaches or flu-like symptoms. I now believe our home environments are the biggest issues.

One other trait about Rodney that I've value ...

He knows his limits.

Each of us does certain things extremely well. But when someone else can do something better than I can, I essentially owe it to whomever I'm serving to bring in that person. The ability of the team is better, which leads to better solutions.

Rodney had me bring in another consultant, John Spears, an architecturally trained designer who specializes in sustainability. John works globally helping entire communities become more sustainable ... looking at housing and heating and power generation and waste management, and also at food. One of John's capabilities is power planning. He showed me how to ...

1. Build a "power budget ... adding up all the uses of power we have in our home, so that we could live a comfortable life. Then ...

2. Look for ways to reduce our power needs, without sacrificing quality of living. The Department of Energy's Web site lists the actual power consumption of appliances. If you want a refrigerator of a certain size and with certain features, you can find them all listed and can see the annual power consumption. You can use compact fluorescent bulbs, which use about 25% of the power of an incandescent bulb. (LED bulbs, which use even less power, didn't exist then.)

3. Third, look at ways not to waste power. For example, closet lights can be designed to go on when the closet door is open, so they're not left on accidentally – or – you can use motion sensors to turn lights off automatically if no one is in the room.

4. Fourth, when you know the amount of power you need to enjoy a comfortable living style, and look at a Local Climatic Data sheet – produced by NOAA (National Oceanographic and Atmospheric Administration,) – to see how many hours of sunshine you get a year.

6. And fifth, find the amount of power produced by a given photovoltaic panel in an hour. Simple math then tells you how many photovoltaic panels you'll need to satisfy 100% of your power needs.

And because the electric grid can go down for an hour or a day or – if a major storm occurs – a few weeks, we also had to plan for reliability …

Power was split into two panel boxes. One included everything we always want on – such as our refrigerator, so food won't spoil, or clocks, so we wouldn't have to reset them each time the grid's down.

Rodney would talk about a 100% passive solar home, meaning that the sun – by itself – would keep you comfortable through the winter. John introduced me to another term, "Net Zero."

During the daylight hours, our photovoltaic panels generate more power than we need. Virginia law requires the power company to buy that surplus power back at the same rate at which it sells it. So – our reversible meter goes backward during daylight hours. Then, when the sun sets – and as we're still using power – we take power back from the grid. In some months, we generate more power than we use, and the utility gives us a credit, which carries over; in some months we use less than we generate. At the end of twelve months, our power bill should be <u>zero</u>.

That expanded my understanding of sustainability.

For each "dimension" – each aspect of sustainability – we need to design our environment to be Net Zero. We also need a storage medium, so we can use that aspect – heating or water or power – *when* we need it. So, for us, the grid is simply a free means of storage for power. When it rains during the night …

We don't need it. When we arise and want to bathe and eat, we do. So – we use cisterns for water storage. In food, tomatoes are abundant when they're ripe and being harvested. But how do we enjoy them the rest of the year?

The two dimensions that don't seem to fit this "Net Zero" and "storage" system are land use – in which we simply try to make the most efficient use of land – and air quality, which we try to keep at as high a level as possible, at all times.

Continuing to other aspects of "drawings" ...

We engaged a Washington, D.C., landscape architect, Scott Fritz, to create a design for our overall site that would contribute to sustainability in additional ways ...

- The Garden Atrium homes would be clustered, using principles of "cluster" or "conservation district" zoning. The overall density – number of houses per acre – remains the same. But individual lots are smaller, and the surplus enables the cluster to have a pond, a boat dock, an orchard, vegetable gardens, and a private park ... more amenities than a typical subdivision ever provides. In addition to land use efficiency, environmental concerns also come into play ...

- The entire site is terraced. Garden Atrium floor levels are at ten feet above mean high tide. Patios are at eight feet. Yards are at six feet. Walkways are five and a half feet. In 90% of the rains, the water simply soaks into the ground. When the occasional heavy downpour occurs, excess water flows into a large pond – which has many times more capacity than code-required stormwater retention areas.

- All areas on which people do not walk use xeriscaping...native plants with a coat of mulch. No irrigation is needed. Maintenance is minimal – a little weeding and new coat of mulch twice a year or so.

- Drives for cars are all permeable, so rainwater stays on site and soaks into the ground – or, in heavy downpours – flows to the pond. No toxic materials, such as blacktop, are used on the site. Paths use small stones, so rain soaks in and no puddles occur. Finally ...

- Aesthetics. Is "aesthetics" truly part of "sustainability"?

It may in fact be. If all environmental factors were satisfied, but if the site – or the home – were not attractive, we're sending a message that we have to sacrifice pleasure to be sustainable. I think sustainability has to include quality-of-life experience. Scott created a Grande Alee' – a 320-foot promenade, flanked by crepe myrtles, flowering shrubs, and 12,000 bulbs. Elegance for "normal" homes.

And for that last aspect of design or "drawings" ...

The plants in the atrium.

With his abilities in landscape design, Scott created a plan for the atrium that provided for a dining area, a sitting area, a water fountain, a hot tub, and an herb garden. But – what specific plants might be best, in which locations?

Using fairly simple logic, I thought about plants that I could grow indoors that I could not grow outdoors. What came to mind was tropical plants ...

- Birds-of-paradise;

- Citrus trees;

- Orchids.

In turns out that citrus trees grow to about ten to twelve feet, which would fit quite comfortably within our Garden Atrium. So ...

Off to "Edible Landscaping," a remarkable nursery southwest of Charlottesville that grew plants that bore some kind of edible product. It provided us with citrus trees for our atrium, trees for our orchard, and berry bushes for the vegetable garden.

For all else, we went to the largest local nursery – which also happens to send a truck to Florida every now and then, to bring back tropical plants. It provided three different birds-of-paradise and a seven-foot-high fountain – which our developer coach wanted us to have, to greet people as they entered. And the nursery provided a huge range of other plants, chosen for their aesthetic diversity ...

- Taller or shorter;

- Different colors; and ...

- Different months for blooming.

With all the drawings and specifications and funding in place ... we began to build the first Garden Atrium home. At the same time, while the first Garden Atrium was being built, we needed to introduce "Cluster Zoning" to Poquoson, which had no such provision. Here, the battle became more formidable ...

Poquoson is a conservative community of about 11,000 that's surrounded by other communities on the peninsula. Most of the homes are ranch style, built in the 1960s and 1970s. Most of the subdivisions are typical of what's done everywhere, which contributes to urban sprawl.

In a conservative community, where people are used to how things have been, people often fear change. Many told us ...

"Why don't you take your ideas to California!"

With our application for a cluster-zoning ordinance, the planning commission was tasked to draft a proposal for the city council. The two city planners were that in title, but neither had a degree in planning. And neither did any research to see what cluster zoning was all about, to educate the lay members of the commission.

In Poquoson, many people interpreted "Cluster Zoning" to mean low-income garden apartments, which would bring in the "wrong types" and increase the crime rate. In fact, all we proposed was keeping the same density of single-family detached homes – but – allowing individual home sites to be smaller, with the extra acreage placed into a "pool" of land, for shared amenities ... a pond, a private park, a boat dock, an orchard, vegetable gardens ... that homeowners don't usually have.

When some commission members recommended a huge setback from the street – which we all knew would place our homes in wetlands, and so would eliminate our project – we asked why they wanted a deeper setback than normal subdivisions.

"So neighbors won't have to look at your house."

When we indicated that neighbors had already been coming to the house – which was now under construction – and really liked what we were doing, they changed their statement to ...

"Well, I drive by and I don't like your home."

When I indicated that all our neighbors had single-story homes with masonry veneers and pitched roofs, and that ours was the same in that regard, and that I didn't understand what there was about the home that was so objectionable ...

"It's different."

This was the first time that I ever saw Trina "lose it." She – and I – walked out of the meeting. They simply saw themselves as a beauty board and had no idea of what cluster zoning was really about. And the municipal planning staff supported their beliefs. No one actually had any formal training or degrees in design or planning, and no one did any research to see what "cluster zoning" really was.

The lessons:

> People seem to fear anything different. And ...

> Because a home is the biggest purchase most of us make, people will more actively and vehemently resist anything that they perceive will diminish the value of their biggest investment. And ...

> Rather than doing any research, to see if a new concept has merits, citizens and municipal staff will reject the idea, out of hand. So ...

Our developer coach, Buddy, suggested I do some research about cluster zoning, and make a presentation at the next city council meeting ... with no more than three recommendations that were different than what the planning commission was recommending. So ...

- I phoned several of my consulting work clients who have serious expertise in cluster zoning. Each gave me more background, and referred me to additional sources, as well.

- I spent many hours Googling. Several articles emerged, all saying positive things about the outcomes of cluster zoning. And ...

- The University of Wisconsin, Milwaukee campus, had done a lot of research into the subject – with verified positive outcomes. Dartmouth University had done the same.

With research compiled from several credible sources, I shared the results of my work with Buddy. Then I began preparing to present to the city council.

Meanwhile, Trina talked to the mayor of Poquoson, who was quite supportive of our project. He suggested that she also speak with the head of the planning commission, who was also sympathetic with our efforts. The mayor and the head of the planning commission each spoke with several of their immediate constituents, and council and commission members, to build behind-the-scenes support.

Buddy would also talk about the many battles he had done with the city over the years, trying to get approval for one project or another. He talked about certain "dissonants" ... local citizens who were quite vocal about their opposition to many of the proposals that came to the city. I suggested we meet with those people and do some listening, in advance of the city council meeting. So ...

- We got the names and address of eleven people who were known for always being at the meetings and quite vocal in their opinions.

- Trina phoned each one of them, and invited them to a meeting ...

- *"We're planning a unique sustainable development, and are looking at a specific site in Poquoson. As people who are active in expressing your opinions, we'd like to share our goals and our designs with you and get your honest reaction. After you hear our ideas ... if you're not comfortable with them, we'll consider trying the project somewhere else. We're not looking to do anything inappropriate."*

- Ten of the eleven activists attended the meeting. They had all seen our initial Garden Atrium going up, but didn't really know what it was all about. They posed questions, made suggestions, and then ...

"<u>This</u> is the type of project we'd like in Poquoson!"

City council meetings are televised. (And – to my amazement – a lot of people actually watch these meetings!) When the floor was open for input, I took the podium and simply shared the research information. Education, with verifiable facts, seems the best way to dispel rumor mills and misconceptions. In fact, one local activist – who's known for opposing many municipal actions – followed my presentation with a round of solid *support* for the cluster-zoning concept. The outcome ...

> Cluster zoning was passed immediately by the city council. (Buddy estimated that it would take two to four years to get it passed.)
>
> And ... Trina was congratulated by many locals at the supermarket. People were amazingly aware of what we were trying to achieve and appreciated the learning that my presentation provided.

It seems that when new ideas are shared and explained, a lot of people are actually open to and appreciate the value of the idea.

Construction problems also arose ...

It seemed to me that if we were creating a new type of home for the 21st century, we might also use new-age electronics as an integral feature of the home ... what's become known as "the smart house." I planned several unique features ...

- Every room was to have cable, phone, and data ports. That way anyone could access the Internet from his or her bedroom, share files with another computer, and use a printer located in another room.

- To cut power waste, motion sensors turn off lights in a vacant room.

- Motions sensors would also turn lights on when someone approaches the front door in the evening, so you never enter a dark home. They would also trigger an alarm if something over a certain size – a potential intruder, not a squirrel – entered a patio after dark.

- And to add a touch of "21st century luxury," voice-activated systems for calling police, for getting an ambulance if a medical problem arose, or for some desired music while you're entertaining. But ...

My ego may have taken me further out than necessary.

Outcomes were mixed.

Specifically ...

- Wiring every room for cable, phone, and data is easily done by the electrician who's doing the other electrical work during construction.

- Motion sensors for controlling lights worked beautifully on the east, north and west sides of the house. However, the photovoltaic panels on the south roof set up an energy field that still allow lights to come on, but not turn off. Smaller motion sensors that cause LED lights under the vanities and kitchen cabinets to come on – so no one has to fumble for a light switch in the dark – do work.

- Outside motion sensors for lighting the entry – inside and outside – at night also work beautifully.

- But the voice-activated touch of 21st century luxury failed miserably. Most of the problem was with the microphones. But we also had real difficulty with the smart-house technical people; they claimed more possibilities than they could deliver. And when it didn't work, they'd suggest remedies that always added cost. After over $50,000 of what felt like wasted expenses, we settled for what worked.

With the exception of the regulatory and smart-house glitches, the Garden Atrium was built, and was a handsome culmination of a sustainability vision! And Trina's initial reticence for this venture, due to the financial risk, evolved into enthusiasm for what became a joint creative effort. Her contribution became significant …

- As she has a bachelor of fine arts in interior design and graphics, she began applying her considerable sensibilities to material selection … such as the type of porcelain tiles that would work best, or recycled wood planks that wore well and looked great, and a stone veneer that most visitors seem to covet.

- She also went through training as an image consultant, which gave her even greater expertise in color sensitivity. While Rodney and I created the basic space concepts, Trina's selection of materials and colors made all the spaces of the house come alive.

- With our design backgrounds, Trina and I tend to be "aesthetic junkies" – we'll buy almost anything that has a striking beauty, from fine art lithographs and etchings, to unique crafts made by artisans in places we've visited, to striking fabrics. Trina displayed our "treasures" in a way that made the Garden Atrium feel like a product of unusually fine quality to the visitors.

Now it was time to see if the concept would sell …

Circa 2002: A Time to Sell

On June 1, 2002, the initial Garden Atrium was complete and open to the public.

Our initial sales strategy involved using the Garden Atrium as a "model home" and building another for someone on one of the remaining six home sites. The question, then, was ...

"How do we get people looking for a new home to visit our model?"

First, our developer-coach, Buddy, encouraged us to bring bagels to the offices of local Realtors, show them our video during their morning sales meeting, and distribute Garden Atrium literature to them. Then, when they'd work with someone looking for a home, they'd bring their client to our model, as an option to consider.

Second, Buddy indicated we'd need to schedule open houses, to attract the public directly. The site he had us acquire was on a busy street, so most locals knew of our project, and the "word" was amazingly spreading ... and quickly.

Third, we sent information, including a video, to newspapers and television stations ... as the homes were truly unique and therefore potentially newsworthy.

And fourth, we created a www.gardenatriums.com Web site. In it, we explained many of the principles of sustainability, showed how the Garden Atrium homes addressed those issues, included a photo tour and the video so people could see the home in 3-D, and invited people to come and tour the model home.

The results of our sales strategy?

First, of the hundreds of Realtors to whom we showed the video and distributed literature, not one phoned us to bring a client through the model home. A few did come by, themselves, to see what the home was like, but none brought potential buyers. Our conclusion is that Realtors prefer to show homes that are within their clients' existing range of expectations, and that have many "comparables" with which to assess the fairness of the asking price. In 2002, no homebuyers would ask their Realtor to find them a Net Zero totally sustainable house.

Second, Buddy wanted our model to be included in a "Roving Parade of Homes" sponsored by the local homebuilders' association. Typically, eight to twelve homes would be on tour from noon to five, Saturday and Sunday, for two consecutive weekends. In this case, June 1st and 2nd, and June 8th and 9th, were the open-house dates. June 1st became our target for completion of the model. Best we could tell, 3,400 people came through the Garden Atrium during those four 5-hour open houses. For most, it was the home's uniqueness. For some, an education.

And the sales outcome?

Nothing.

A few found the home *"Just too different."* Most actually enjoyed the feel of the home. But with the huge turnout, our ability to get to know anyone and respond to questions about how the home heated and cooled and powered and watered itself, etc., was severely limited. We could answer a few questions as people flowed past, and that was about all. Time to build relationships was too limited.

Over the coming months, however, we conducted open houses every Saturday and Sunday afternoon, placing ads in the local paper. On average, we had roughly thirty to fifty people see the house each day. We did have more time to speak with people and explain what the house did. Out of that effort came a few prospects.

We worked with three or four couples that seemed genuinely intrigued, and were looking for a new home in Poquoson. (It turns out that Poquoson's small school system consistently tops out on statewide school ratings. Excellent schools are a major homebuyer attractor.)

So … consistently large open house turnouts, but no buyers.

Meanwhile …

One mile away, on the same road, Buddy completed a condo project for active seniors. All 88 units – costing about $225,000 each – sold out in five hours! Buyers literally stood in line with checks in their hands.

I asked Buddy why the huge difference in our sales performance. His response …

1. The Hampton Roads area – southeastern Virginia – has a steady in-migration of active seniors. He targets that group.

2. His designs are more traditional, so they're not an issue for buyers. They just look at the different floor plans, consider the special amenities they'd like … and make a buying decision.

3. Real estate is like a Christmas tree. How many in an area can afford a $3 million home? A $1 million home? $700,000? $225,000? The lower the cost, the larger the group of potential buyers. Our Garden Atrium – because I didn't want the atrium to feel like a postage stamp – was large, at 4928 sq ft, and would cost a million to build.

4. Each model condo he had was already built, and professionally furnished. Some people won't wait five to eight months for construction of a custom home, so he had units already available.

From the third aspect of our sales strategy, sending information to the media, we were, in fact, widely publicized …

We were featured in local papers and in the *Washington Post*. We appeared as a special on the evening news of two major local TV stations. Those efforts caused a steady flow of interested visitors when we had our open houses – including over two hundred couples from the Washington, D.C., area. But ... none bought.

From the fourth aspect of our sales strategy, a Web site, we did have – and continue to have – a heavy and steady amount of traffic. We receive inquiries from all over the U.S. ... and from other countries, as well. It's amazing. One professional society contacted us and said that we may have the *most* sustainable homes east of the Mississippi. (Flattering, but it doesn't say much for our country's progress.)

Web site inquiries led to hundreds of e-mail dialogues. Many eventually came to see the home. Photographing. Lots of "oohs" and "aahs." But ... no sales.

After several months, we concluded that our strategy was giving us great exposure and a huge volume of people who were interested in sustainability or in the uniqueness of the Garden Atrium concept. But none of the interest was crystallizing into sales. So we asked Buddy for his suggestion ...

> *"As much as it might stress you financially, you need to design and build – 'on spec' – a Garden Atrium that is less than half the size and cost of the initial model. The cost would fit within the budgets of many more people. And people could tour the home, learn about the systems, and then either leave or ... buy it and move in ... within <u>weeks</u>."*

He also made some suggestions that he thought would make the design more comfortable to people ...

- Instead of the brick pavers in the atrium of the model, go to poured concrete and porcelain tiles. Same thermal mass, with better insulation. Same cost, but a more finished look – like a "great room."

- Instead of the porcelain tiles used as base moldings in the model, go to wood ... for a warmer, more "homey" look.

- Make the reverse osmosis filter, solid wood cabinetry, zero VOC paints, dye-free wool carpeting, rainwater cisterns, and even photovoltaic power and solar hot water "amenity upgrades." That way, our base price would be a lot lower, and everyone buys the upgrades.

> *"That's how new homes are sold."*

I agreed to all of his suggestions – except those that defined the home as sustainable. So ... fireplaces and granite counter-tops could readily be amenity upgrades. But the solar power and hot water, and the water and air purification systems, had to be standard. And that began a new chapter in our journey ...

Circa 2004: The Qu Fu is Born

Many subdivisions in the United States use British names ... the Buckingham Estates" for a development of modest ranch-style homes. I suppose it's a marketing effort, to add prestige to more modest housing than the real Buckingham Palace. I thought about great structures in the world that featured atriums, and used their names to perhaps more appropriately match a name with a design.

For the initial Garden Atrium model, with a large 35 ft x 35 ft atrium, I thought of historic structures with large atriums. On Crete, one of the great palaces built by the Minoans was at Phaistos. In its center is a grand atrium courtyard surrounded by marble columns. While our model isn't exactly of that scale, it is equally grand, so we named the first Garden Atrium the Phaistos Model.

Now we needed something smaller – more intimate. A home with atriums that fit that sensibility is located in eastern China, in Qu Fu (pronounced Choo Foo).

The home was owned by the Kong family, who were governors of the province (before the formation of a single "China" in 232 BC) Around 450 BC, the head of the family began taking cross-cultural trips .. long expeditions to learn what he could from other cultures. (Not easy to do in those days.) When he returned to Qu Fu, he'd share his learnings. Eventually, he became know as "Kong, the Great Teacher." The Chinese word for "great teacher" is Foo' Dzuh, so he became known as "Kong Fudzuh" ... which the missionaries evolved into "Confucius."

When you visited the governor in those days, there was no motel across the street, so the Kongs were obliged to provide guest quarters. Adjacent to each guest room is a small atrium garden, often with a stone bench and a small cluster of bamboo, and sometimes a little trickling fountain. Intimate, quiet, serene, pleasant. So ... we named our smaller Garden Atrium the "Qu Fu."

To reduce the square footage, we eliminated the hallway that separated the surrounding rooms from the garden. While it's nice to look into a garden from a place of shelter, it's also a lot of square footage. In the Qu Fu, you walk from a surrounding room directly into the atrium ... which is still quite comfortable.

We also reduced the size of the Qu Fu Atrium, from 35 ft. x 35 ft. to 28 ft. x 28 ft. It was still 784 sq. ft. ... not as large as the Phaistos atrium, but still more than "ample" ... and larger than the size of most great rooms.

We also changed the roof. In Phaistos, we used a symmetrically pitched glass skylight. As solar radiation bounces, a symmetrical roof is not as efficient as when the south-facing glass is a perfect 90° to the winter sun ... to maximize insolation.

Rodney also initiated one other roof adjustment ...

The north slope of the atrium roof was now opaque. Two layers of glass, even with argon gas between them, achieves an insulating value of only R-16 or so. By shifting to an opaque roof, the north-facing roof achieved an insulating value of R-56.

As skylights are quite expensive, the new roof – with a south-facing skylight, glass to the east and west, and an opaque roof to the north – was a lot less expensive. So – the new roof achieved greater efficiency at less cost ... and still had the "open-to-the-sky" feeling, and the flood of daylight that distinguishes Garden Atriums.

The room sizes surrounding the atrium remained the same. The master bedroom suite – loved by most visitors – remained precisely the same. And the kitchen's island, with range and overhead rack – another valued feature – remained the same.

We implemented Buddy's suggestion of continuing the porcelain tiles into the atrium. They gave the space a more "finished" look, and they require no maintenance. In the areas for plants, we placed a soaker hose, operated by a timer. That way, the plants are watered even when the owners forget – or are on vacation.

For those of you who've gone through the process of purchasing a home ...

> *"How did you feel when you left the closing meeting?"*

Typically, you're tired of signing scores of forms. You often have almost nothing left in your bank accounts. And you see payments on a large mortgage in your future. Now, while you're feeling that sense of poverty, imagine beginning a second home and facing payments on a second mortgage! But, we were committed. So ...

We began constructing a second Garden Atrium, the Qu Fu, on spec. And ...

When construction was complete, and when we received our Certificate of Occupancy ... we had <u>three</u> contract offers!

Fantastic!

Designing a Net Zero sustainable home isn't really that difficult. The technology is constantly being refined, but it's been around for some time. The real test is marketability. Can a Garden Atrium compete with traditional housing, so that it might eventually become mainstream, and make a difference? When I asked all three couples who made contract offers why they did so, they all had the same reasons:

1. *"It's gorgeous!"* Aesthetics clearly topped the list.

2. *"It's really well built – real wood, not plastic."* And ...

3. *"The notion of lower utility bills is appealing."*

Some conclusions ...

I was curious that the people making the two contract offers we could not accept would not wait six or seven months for us to build another home for them. Evidently, when people want a new home, many want it *now*.

People also didn't really believe that Net Zero was possible. And – even though we showed them actual utility bills from the initial Garden Atrium – they only believed they'd have a slight reduction in utility cost, and would have to see for themselves.

None of the people offering contracts were "environmental zealots." And visitors who said they had huge environmental concerns really appreciated what we had done – but none of them made a contract offer. No one is really against sustainability; it's like "motherhood." But that isn't what motivated buyers.

What I discovered was:

I might build Garden Atriums for one reason, but ...

People were buying them for their own reasons.

Nonetheless, our euphoria – partly from our sales success and partly from coming out of a deep state of indebtedness – led us to quickly begin *two* more Qu Fu Garden Atriums – also on spec. The bank gave us the construction loans, and we were ready to ...

"Strike while the iron is hot."

What I've found almost invisible is the awareness the public has about a project – at least about our project. Seeing the second Garden Atrium sell so quickly, and now seeing two more under construction, sends a message that maybe this kind of home isn't so crazy after all. They began seeing it as ...

"The way of the future."

With no promotional effort to seek publicity, we were regularly published as feature articles in local and regional magazines. Inquiries from our Web site continued; I probably take two to four families a week through the home, just from inquiries. And the open houses – now scheduled about once a month – continued to have strong turnout. While our developer coach might have four couples visit one of his developments over a weekend, we might have fifty. But ...

He still made more sales!

And as the next two Garden Atriums were completed, the site also took on a different character ...

- Wood privacy fences connect the homes. Every bedroom has a private patio. Kids are able to play in total safety, and ...

...not have to clean up as carefully. Connecting the homes also pre-
vents kids and pets from running into the street – or strangers from
coming on site and using the site amenities.

- The landscape design became more evident, as plantings matured.
  The 320-foot Grande Allee was becoming elegant. For instance ...

- By now, we'd planted over 12,000 bulbs, so you can see color even
  in February. The hypericum plants provided a two-foot-high flow of
  yellow flowers from April to November. The crepe myrtles provided a
  tunnel of pink flowers for two to three months every summer. And the
  Knockout roses, at squares where paths crossed, provided color and
  scent until December. People could begin to see that they could live
  sustainably, and also live elegantly.

- Building codes require what's known as BMP (Best Management Practices.) It's a method for capturing rainwater, so sediments settle and
  purer water flows from the site. In most developments, you'll see a
  grassy dent in the ground. In architecture school, I learned that if we
  faced what seemed a nuisance, we should convert it into a feature. We
  created a large pond, with a gazebo in the middle – reached by a bridge –
  a solar powered fountain, and water lilies.

- Surrounding the pond we planted an orchard – apples, pears, peaches,
  cherries, plums, apricots, and figs. It's amazing how people don't
  know when a piece of fruit is ripe, or that they can eat it right from
  the tree. (We also had to learn how to share our orchard's abundance
  with birds and raccoons – part of sustainable living.)

- The park – flat land with mature trees and grass lawn – was 250 feet
  across, and more defined; people began using it. Grass lawns are
  high-maintenance elements, but they're the best surfaces for people to
  walk on. Except for the private park, the site was xeriscaped.

- The boat dock enabled us to harbor a 17-foot sailboat, and take it out
  on Chesapeake Bay ... as our site is only half a mile from it. The dock
  is also a great place for "birding," as the area is rife with Great Blue
  herons, Snowy White egrets, and mallards.

- And the vegetable gardens began to flourish. Each year, with composting, the soil become richer and yielded better results. Kids showed the
  greatest enthusiasm, when their plants grew and they could harvest
  beans, peas, corn, carrots ... or berries, from bushes.

As the site matured, so did I. I began to experience sustainability as more than a way
to cut carbon emissions and save on utility bills. I began to see the site as a key, in
that it helps us to begin ...

... living *with* nature, not conquer it, and actually enjoy our environment even *more*. I never had a back-yard that provided what we now have.

So, two more Qu Fu Garden Atriums moved toward completion. Our site became more mature, more elegant, and more useful.. The interest in what we were doing grew. And we enjoyed a lot of visitors at our open houses. Then ...

The real estate market died.

As the financial market fell apart and the economy faltered, real estate sales dried up. Major housing developers went out of business or merged with a more solvent developer. And many retirees who wanted to move into the Hampton Roads area could not do so as readily, because they couldn't sell their current home.

When the next two Qu Fu Garden Atriums were complete, interest was high – they are truly lovely homes. But offers didn't come. So ... we rented them to families who preferred rental housing. (Many military families prefer to rent for a year or so when they're transferred to a new area, to get the lay of the land.) The two families may convert the homes to a purchase, after a year or two or three. But until then, they pay rent, and we pay the difference between the rent and the mortgage.

Despite the slow market, we were still committed to completing this initial sustainable housing project. And open-house attendance remained strong, as interest in sustainability has been growing considerably since the start of our project. But ...

We certainly couldn't build the remaining three home sites on spec.

Our sales strategy shifted.

I show our home – the original Garden Atrium – and explain all the principles of sustainability. (In fact, our home has become kind of a classroom, in which people can "see and feel" things they only read about. Visitors also see the site and the exterior of the Qu Fu homes. Then, if visitors express interest ...

1. I arrange for them to go through one of the Qu Fu homes. (Residents are quite proud to show off their Garden Atriums.) We also ask them to note "likes and dislikes" as they do so.

2. Then I sit down with them, listen to their preferences, and create a modification of the Qu Fu that fits their needs as ideally as possible – without affecting any of the sustainable elements.

3. After two or three meetings, when the couple is delighted with their home's design, I ask our contractor to distill a price for building it. And then ...

4. If the couple loves the home and finds the cost workable, then – after they think about it – we sell them one of the remaining home sites at their appraised value, and charge them a fee for the plans.

This process reduces the overall cost of the home to the homebuyer. It enables us to tweak the design, to fit their living preferences most closely. And it reduces our indebtedness, as each site is sold.

The fifth Garden Atrium was completed that way. During monthly open houses, we're experiencing interest in the two remaining home sites; it seems a matter of time until this first sustainable housing project will be complete.

There are many "lessons learned" from living in a Garden Atrium ...

- The heating, cooling, power generation, and rainwater harvesting systems worked beautifully. Utility bills were ridiculously low, but we didn't necessarily hit Net Zero, as residents don't necessarily live within design assumptions ... desired temperatures or power use.

- Stay with technology that has local support and supports sustainability and quality-of-life experience; forget the exotics – e.g., smart-home technology – that increase cost and don't help sustainability.

- Have patience with regulators. The fifth Garden Atrium went off grid on water, using a well for backup. While the state health department officials turned out to be interested in sustainability and wonderfully supportive, municipal regulators presented difficulties – which I had to bring in an attorney to resolve. New designs seem to make many regulators nervous; they don't seem to like making decisions when a long-term, proven track record doesn't exist.

- Air quality was an unexpected positive. Initially, I selected plants for aesthetic reasons. When someone commented that they might improve air quality, we hired a toxicologist to measure it. Our indoor air had about the same CO_2 as outdoors and much higher oxygen levels. And from a book, *How to Grow Clean Air,* by a NASA researcher, we found that the simple Boston fern was great at removing toxins. Residents reported allergies vanishing in days.

- In a "tight" solar house, with minimal infiltration, the moisture given off by the plants can create mold problems, if relative humidity exceeds 65%. We use Energy Recovery Ventilators to control that.

- My eyes got stronger. As we age, eyes usually need more prescription. My eyes equalized in strength, my astigmatism vanished, and both eyes needed less prescription (– which still cost money!) Why?

- Daylighting. It's much easier on the eyes. We don't need to turn on any lights until it's dark outside, because the homes have an enormous flood of natural – and healthful – daylight. Daylighting also eliminates problems many have with Seasonal Affective Disorder.

- Homebuyers compare options on a house-price-per-square-foot basis. We need to have them compare homes on a cost-per-square-foot basis for mortgage *and* utilities, to be "apples to apples"; it's a big paradigm shift.

- The glass walls separating bedrooms from the atrium were initially suspect to many, even with curtains. Later, residents reported that they spent more time together as a family, in the atrium. And ...

- On the more unusual side, people – kids and adults – seem to connect more to the sun and moon and stars and the earth's rhythm.

As Garden Atrium #5 was moving toward completion and as we held open houses to entice someone to begin #6, I began wondering what we had <u>not</u> included in this first effort. For instance, in relation to food ...

- I cited the 1997 notice that China had become a net food importer. And the trend article indicating China had a 25-year straight-line decline in food production, and that because of China's size, by 2016 (best case) the world would not have sufficient surplus to sell them. (In 2003, China's food imports equaled Canada's entire harvest.)

- The initial Garden Atrium development has a vegetable garden and an orchard. But the percent of residents' total food needs that could be satisfied by what was on our site would be insignificant. We provided tasteful and healthy treats, but not the majority of staples.

- Global water shortages have continued to escalate, with water wars likely between countries that each need water from the same rivers.

- Our population is trending towards eating more fish, and the oceans are being fished out; demand is growing as supply is vanishing.

- And by the end of 2007, over 40 million people a year were dying of starvation, alone. And the annual number is growing.

Without apologizing whatever for what we'd begun, sustainable living would evidently have to go a lot further. As an architect, I thought mostly about physical elements – housing and site development – not about food, or other factors that might be just as vital to living sustainably. And that led to expansive research ...

Entrance to Phaistos Garden Atrium

Atrium from kitchen, Phaistos Garden Atrium

Atrium from Master bedroom

Kitchen island, Phaistos Garden Atrium

Atrium from Phaistos dining room

Atrium from kitchen, Qu Fu Garden Atrium

Pedestrian side of Garden Atriums; rooftop PV panels

The Grande Allee'

Pond from Qu Fu Garden Atrium

Qu Fu Garden Atrium, across pond

Circa 2007: A Look at Sustainable Living

Since the beginning of my journey – which gradually evolved from "sustainable housing" to "sustainable living" – several major changes have occurred ...

- In 2006-7, we reached "Global Peak Oil." The impact this will have on transportation, power supply, and food will be enormous!

- Pew Research recently completed a study indicating that public confidence in long-trusted institutions is low and getting lower. Our confidence that government, at any level, can solve any of these sustainability problems is dropping lower than it's ever been.

- Aging municipal infrastructures, which lead to collapsing bridges, bursting mains, towns running out of water, potholes – along with disruptions of utility services – are becoming more frequent and apparent. And agencies seem to be short of maintenance funds.

- The influence of nation-states – our civilization's global organization – as well as the leaders of those nations, has been dropping. Multinational corporations seem to have more influence on how we live. However, their goal is profitability, not sustainability.

To whom do we then turn to help us out of so enormous a bind as "sustainability"?

We are all part of a system ...our civilization. I don't believe that anarchy will have the connectedness to solve sustainability issues. And I don't think running into the woods to survive will contribute to our civilization's evolution. I think sustainability will have to be solved by a large number of small, "grassroots" efforts ... each contributing to an evolving larger solution for mankind. Accordingly ...

I believe my next effort will have to be unconnected to any grid – other than the Internet, for global communication. I believe homes need to be smaller and more affordable, as this approach may be the only way people who are not wealthy will be able to sustain ... and can enjoy a high "quality-of-life" experience.

We're all dependent on the social, economic, and governmental systems in which we live. Good or bad, it's all we know. To ease the transition from what's familiar and comfortable – but clearly not sustainable – to a system that is sustainable and maybe even more comfortable, we need to experience another alternative. Not hear about it or read about it ... *experience* it. Then we all might be able to say ...

"This is really <u>nice</u>!"
"I can easily live this way."

A 2nd generation sustainable development must provide that positive model. So ...

Based on our experience with the Garden Atrium project, Trina and I brainstormed what we called "dimensions" … nine factors that we believe need to be addressed to create an environment that is sustainable in <u>all</u> senses … physical, social, educational, cultural, spiritual … everything and anything that's needed that would cause residents to enjoy and proclaim a high quality of life experience.

In our initial Garden Atrium development, we're both developers and neighbors. I dread people feeling "buyer's remorse." And I can say that the residents who are here really *like* living here. In fact, when being interviewed by a reporter from a local newspaper, one of the residents said (paraphrasing) …

> *"When my husband and I visit friends, then leave their house and get back in our car, we look at each other and say, 'We can't go back!' This is a house I never want to leave."*

That's a benchmark. I'd like our next venture to go even *further.* And while so much of the "green" movement focuses on clean, renewable energy and more efficient cars, the ultimate measure of success can't be a lack of utility bills. It has to be happiness … fulfillment … great quality-of-life feelings … residents who are delighted to be living there and who would never want to return to the "old ways."

The nine dimensions I began exploring are:

1. Community.

2. Health care.

3. Food.

4. Leisure.

5. Transportation.

6. Education.

7. Trade.

8. Internet.

9. Infrastructure.

In the past two years, another phenomenon – or "dimension" – has surfaced, which may be even more characterizing of the transition that's occurring in civilization. I'll save that for after I've shared what I learned about these first nine dimensions.

The research I did involved extensive reading of books and articles, considerable Internet exploring, and interviews with specialists. I'll cite sources as I go. So …

Community

Many people have recently written about emerging living trends, especially related to sustainability. Here are some. The flow is choppy, but a theme does emerge.

"Local Techers," one of Barker and Erickson's groups in *Five Regions of the Future,* prefer small to big, but don't focus on size for its own sake. A village is a model for human development. Not too big, or dehumanizing. Not too small, either, or we'll miss the richness of variety in life. Scale is the key. Proper scale is what humans can effectively manage in any environment. In a "Local Tech" region, we'll live in ...

> **Human-scaled villages and communities, with technology that helps us use the resources of nature in a way that protects the planet and allows us to work in a way that fully develops our humanity.** The essence: **"Small and local is beautiful."**

Next, here's an excerpt from Joel Garreau's *"Radical Evolution"* ...

> *"Much later it occurs to me that Felipe Mendoza's world is a metaphor for Prevail. It is this intensely local yet vastly global arrangement that's very complex and very authentic whose pivot literally is flavor.*
>
> *"Mendoza is no poster child for going back to some static nature, Lanier observes. Mendoza talks about all the varieties of chilis they are experimenting with to see how far they can push their business. His livelihood depends upon people coming to Hatch (NM) and saying Hatch is special. He is both a man of the world and is grounded in that place. He is clearly somebody who has the flavor of the valley.*
>
> *"He is the essence of being connected while relishing differences."*

Mendoza has a chili restaurant in Hatch, New Mexico. Garreau believes localities need authenticity to maintain a true local character, and that such character is valued.

The pattern that's emerging seems something like the bumper sticker ...

> ***"Think globally, but live locally."***

Referring to Michael H. Shuman, in *"Going Local"* ...

> *"To succeed in a world of shifting loyalties, a community going local must simultaneously retain a global perspective."*

"The Rule of 150" is another concept of historic importance ...

Evidently due to the size of the human brain cortex, we can generally maintain about 150 relationships – at a level at which we truly care about people, and will walk over to greet or join them when we see them. Bill Gore built his Gore-Tex company around that rule, so no building or division exceeded 150. The idea: if people care about one another, they'll make the company work. Religious sects also revolved – consciously or not – around that 150-person size limit. Above that number, sects and villages and company divisions would routinely subdivide.

Using the 150-person maximum as a rule, and with the average number of households having 2.2 people ...

A sustainable village maximum should be sixty-eight homes.

The Rule of 150 is quantitative, the maximum number allowed to maintain a true sense of "community." But some small towns are "pits," while others are "happening places." In tests, the dimension, "social capital," consistently parallels perceptions of "quality of life." Social capital seems largely influenced by the degree to which people feel they can shape or influence their community ... empowerment.

Using my personal experience as a group facilitator, techniques – such as "Synthesizing Triads" – can be used to gain a true consensus, even from large groups and in a fairly short amount of time. In the process, people are asked to get into a group of three – triads. Then a problem or question is posed, such as ...

"What amenities should be available in the village?"

Groups of three are wonderfully efficient. Even normally quiet people will participate – often with excellent ideas. Triads can come up with a solution to most problems or questions within twenty to thirty minutes. If the issue is sensitive, then ...

*"Please get with two other people with whom you have
a comfortable relationship."*

If the issue may be best approached through a diverse range of opinions, then ...

"Please get with two people you really don't know."

After twenty to thirty minutes, each triad selects a representative and the other two leave. Then ...

*"Please meet with two other representatives. Share your ideas with
them, and listen to theirs. Then, create a single solution that embodies everything you have in yours – a solution you know the two people
you're representing would favor."*

After another twenty to thirty minutes, repeat the same process, until you have only one triad and one solution. Does this system work?

I've used this process with considerable success in addressing a variety of issues in organizations. That process will be tested in the Homeowners' Association of the first Garden Atrium project.

What the Synthesizing Triads process replaces is …

"Robert's Rules of Order."

We've been conditioned to this process since high school. Yet, it's more of a control process than a means for engaging large numbers of people that make up a community. In order to increase social capital – the degree to which people feel they can influence their own community – we need processes that engage them … without frustrating them. Synthesizing Triads is one such process. The aim …

Participation … not representation.

Here's another thought from *"Radical Evolution"* that is key to sustainable living …

> *"You can't have modern democracy … unless you have this basic belief in equality, which means that you should empathize with suffering and feelings of other people and recognize their rights as equal to your own."*

Garreau's concern is: divisions between what he calls The Enhanced, The Naturals, and The Rest may be so profound as to make past ruptures over race and religion seem quaint and paltry. This attitude – along with a total involvement, consensus-based governance process – seems essential. One other supporting thought…

> *"Dependency, especially on political and religious authority, is the distinguishing mark of a barbarous and primitive society, while autonomy – liberty – is the mark of a modern and civilized one."*
> Arthur Herman.

Now we're talking about a huge difference between how our current system of governance works and how we'll need to govern ourselves in a community focused on sustainable living. And from Shuman's *"Going Local,"* we add …

> *"The larger a political entity, the more difficulty a citizen has identifying with or caring about his or her neighbors. For people to have a meaningful feeling of community, they need to know, communicate, work with, and trust their neighbors."*

The more people are *directly involved* in making decisions that govern their lives, the stronger their confidence in themselves, their neighbors, and their community to solve problems that come along. This is a huge difference from how we live now!

One day I was wondering if anyone or any company focused its effort on making a community more exciting. I Googled. And up came one company's Web site, the Planning and Design Institute, a Milwaukee firm. Its stated focus …

Making small communities exciting places in which to live.

The staffs' professional backgrounds are in planning, architecture, and landscape architecture, and their focus is essential – though rather unusual. From my interview with three principals, here are some guidelines for making a community a lively and rewarding environment in which to live. The primary key is ...

Shared public experience.

People need a <u>reason</u> to use a space that, in turn, causes elbow rubbing. People will go to *active* coffee houses, to share experiences with others, which led them to suggest the idea of a central inn. Some uses that are proven to work include ...

- A spa, sauna, etc.;

- An exercise room, perhaps with lap pool;

- A central "post office" – for mail, UPS and FedEx packages;

- And equestrian trails – whether they own or rent a horse for a ride.

Other possible uses that are likely to work equally well might include ...

- An orchard – tending to fruit;

- Winter gardening, in a greenhouse;

- Health care, provided once a week, at the inn;

- Walking ...especially through a hardwood forest;

- Planning, preparing, and enjoying gourmet food;

- A winery – many people enjoy making their own wine;

- Personal storage: walking to it, like having a giant closet;

- Repairing – going to a shop, with tools provided, to fix things;

- Art – studios for pottery, drawing, painting, weaving, sculpting;

- Kinko's-type service – services or products provided at the inn;

- And concierge service – provided by the inn, and including a huge range of services for residents. This idea at first seemed odd, but now I see it as *essential*. Services can include ...

Dry cleaning; securing tickets for events; pizza delivery; watering plants or walking or feeding pets while on vacation; providing greeting cards; buying desired groceries or other readily specified items.

Services surrounding a concierge cause a huge information exchange among residents. The concierge should also be a "people" person, who likes to get to know people, and their interests and hobbies, and does matchmaking ...

> *"You work in pottery? Jenny Smith and David Johnston also do a lot of work in pottery. If you like, I can introduce you to them. Could be a positive coincidence for all of you."*

Or ...

> *"You're looking to learn how to can tomatoes? I think Marian McCarver knows a lot about that, and is going to teach it to some of the others. Would you like me to introduce you to her?"*

Activities should occur near a "crossroads" – which can be the lobby of the inn, or an outdoor square near the inn, etc. (At this point the concept of having an inn was emerging as being critical to being able to create a true sense of "community.")

Spaces that accommodate living, working, *and* playing add excitement.

And some activities will evolve incrementally, from residents – such as pottery or chess playing or winemaking or gourmet cooking. The development needs to have a way of accommodating such interests as they surface. It could involve creating indoor or outdoor chess tables, studios for various artisans, or a space adjacent to a well-equipped kitchen for teaching gourmet cooking – or other classes.

Another key factor influencing the quality of life is: **happiness!**

According to an ABC News special, five major factors increase happiness ...

Close and supportive relationships between people is the first and likely the biggest predictor of happiness. Happiness expert Prof. David Myers states simply ...

> *"Close, supportive, and connected relationships make for happiness.*
>
> *"Social support – feeling liked, affirmed, and encouraged by intimate friends and family – promotes both health and happiness. A friend is someone with whom you feel comfortable being yourself. Friends enable us to be known and accepted as we truly are."*

According to Prof. Myers, short of torture, society's worst punishment is solitary confinement. People want companions. We seek others to do things with and to share the experience of being human. Companionship combats loneliness and promotes well-being. Friends often exchange favors in helping each other meet the demands of ordinary living. It's a big plus. If we have a friend, then ...

We can count on our friend for help when the rough spots in life occur.

The "Rule of 150," the opportunities for people to meet and cultivate relationships – at crossroads and in shared activities – and direct participation in governance of the community should increase residents' actual feelings of happiness.

At this point, my sense about what constituted "sustainability" began to evolve. If I created a community that was an "environmentally friendly" model, but in which the residents were not delighted to be there, I'd be embarrassed. I think "sustaining" has to be more than "surviving." When people are happy and satisfied, they will more easily connect with one other and with nature – the earth. This begins and enhances sustainability. Actually ... it is at the *heart* of sustainability.

The second happiness factor, work, comes when we test our skills through some meaningful activity. Happiness increases if the work is fulfilling. And ...

How do we describe "fulfilling" work?

"Flow" describes a work situation in which a person is totally absorbed in the activity, to the point at which hours pass without the person realizing it. An artist works for hours on a piece of art, being absorbed the whole while in the act of creation, and finding the whole experience very rewarding. "Flow" occurs when a person is using his or her highest skills in doing work he or she finds challenging. Flow experiences boost our sense of self-esteem, competence, and well-being.

A key ingredient of satisfying work is whether it is challenging. The most satisfied workers find their skills tested, their work varied, their tasks "significant." As a sustainable community is not necessarily work-related, the only support that I could think of that could help in this dimension is a process known as executive coaching ... helping people – even successful leaders – identify "meaningfulness."

The third key happiness factor is the level of **"personal control"** a person has over his or her life. "Control theory" distinguishes between an internal and an external locus of control.

- An internal locus of control is a belief that life outcomes are largely the result of our own attributes and behaviors.

- An external locus of control is the belief that outcomes are largely determined by factors and forces outside our control.

People with an external locus of control are more susceptible to depression, learned helplessness, a sense of victimization, and negative responses to aversive stimuli. People with an internal locus of control tend to be happier. The "Synthesizing Triads" consensus model, for making decisions governing the community, should provide a considerable boost to residents' internal locus of control. And the fourth happiness factor is ...

Optimism!

Author John Powell states that research points to a common denominator among people who are happy. They are "Goodfinders." They look for and find what is good in themselves, others, and in all situations in life. Consider this contrast:

> *"Two men looked out from prison bars.*
> *One saw mud and one saw stars."*

Looking for good enables brighter feelings; we can usually find something good in other people and things if we try. And if things aren't perfect, or are seemingly unacceptable, we may find there are redeeming characteristics found in the existing good amidst the flaws. If Powell is right, we may find ourselves smiling more often as we look for the good in other people and in things ... or in ourselves.

Not much in the community fabric will necessarily build (or hurt) optimism.

And the fifth key happiness factor is spiritual faith. Where there's spiritual hunger, there's a forthcoming emotional sustenance from spirituality. Are spiritually committed people happier than those who aren't? According to Gallup polls ... yes!

"The highly spiritual were <u>twice</u> as likely to say they were 'very happy.'"

The community's likely food source, CSA farming, will be biodynamic ... a system developed by clairvoyant Rudolph Steiner. Ideas from Findhorn, and from Machaelle Small Wright's co-creation work at Perelandra, will likely be a factor for bringing human and nature spirit energy together. Other than providing a positive environment for "connecting," for meditation, or for dialogue, a sustainable community is not a religious community, per se, so nothing in the fabric *necessarily* is likely to bolster (or diminish) spirituality or religious followings among residents.

Those five factors, from research, seem most vital to giving residents happiness ... a high-quality-of-life feeling. In terms of how a sense of community can be created by the design of the site, some thoughts from the Planning and Design Institute ...

Either locate the village and inn at the entry from the road, with the farm structures as a distant "polar opposite," or locate the farm structures at the entry – and create an "entrance through a farm hamlet" experience – with the village and inn across the farmland, as a polar opposite. If the latter, consider ...

- The inn, which is a larger structure than the individual houses, needs high visibility – "eye candy" – a powerful, commanding design.

- The road across the farm fields to the village needs to be a ...

"Napoleonic" road ... narrow, with evenly spaced trees symmetrically lining both sides of the road ... and focused on the strong visual statement created by the inn and village. (This style of road was actually designed by Napoleon, for his armies.)

- Houses in the village need especially nice garage doors, to help set and reinforce a statement of character for the village.

We all talk about wanting to be in a sense of community. Few, however, describe exactly what that means. If "Sustainability" – or better, "Sustainable living " – needs to be rewarding, then these ideas become certainly relevant.

Next, the second dimension on which I did research ...

Health Care

Clinicians need to see 105 patients a week. The villages of 150, that we're describing, are clearly too small to even support a clinic. A town of 500 or so might support a part-time chiropractor, and that's three times the size we're planning. So ...

The villages need to be within, say, 20 miles of a medical center. That way, a variety of medical services can be available within half an hour. Trips to a larger community that has a medical center can be shared, so that if gas is used, the per-person cost is reasonable. Most electric cars can go 65 to 120 miles on a single charge, and so they can also make the 20-mile round trip, easily and economically.

The inn would likely need a van, to support concierge services. That van – arranged through the concierge, as another service – could provide transportation.

Looking longer term, I imagine a number of small villages such as we're describing. If I see them as a network, then physicians could simply be serving a network whose total population will support that medical practice. This pattern is also consistent with the Barker & Erickson book ...

> *"Treat people locally, when possible, and moved to medical centers only when needed. Individual care in small settings is the best kind of healthcare, anyway. With information, diagnosis, and skill provided through the Web, treatment can be as effective in small local settings as in large medical centers."*

> *"Local Techers also embrace the use of edible medicinal plants, even though herbal plants, until recently, have been largely shunned by Western science ... Local Techers utilize plants and plant extracts from their locally grown flora to counter illness and disease."*

The third dimension of sustainability in which I did research is ...

Food

Several stable trends point to potential issues in feeding our global population ...

1. Desertification. Every year, we lose farmland the size of Rhode Island to desert.

2. We've unquestionably passed Peak Oil, at least functionally. Every day, there is less oil available, per person, on the planet ... which puts us into a "lifeboat" exercise – ten people in a boat designed for eight – or wars. We can drive fewer miles in more efficient cars, but agribusiness uses oil-based pesticides and fertilizers. Before the Industrial Revolution, we fed 650 million; we have over ten times that now. It isn't sustainable, even with better seeds and farm practices.

3. We're running out of water. The world's largest aquifer, the Ogallala, under the Midwestern States, is a third of what it was, and is not rechargeable. India and Pakistan over-pump their aquifers; their water tables are dropping 1.5 meters a year. Kashmir, in the headlands to the Himalayas, has two huge rivers, and India and Pakistan's real fight is over who controls the water. China has two main rivers, the Yangtze and the Yalu; the Yalu has been dry at least one month a year for almost 20 years – with accompanying crop failures.

According to WorldWatch Institute ...

> *"Satisfying the food demands of the growing human population while at the same time sustaining freshwater and terrestrial ecosystems presents enormous challenges. Already, as much as 10 percent of global food production depends on the overpumping of groundwater. In India, where millions of wells have run dry, that figure is closer to 25 percent. These hydrologic deficits create a bubble in the food economy that is bound to burst, and they raise questions about where the additional water needed for future food production will come from."*

Desalinization is now inexpensive. Constructing pipelines to the central parts of countries for irrigation purposes is incredibly costly (and can take decades.)

4. I mentioned that, in 1997, China announced it was importing food for the first time in its history. I cited its 25-year straight-line decline in food production that simply crossed from diminishing exports to the start of imports that year. And because of China's size, the rest of the world will not have enough surplus to sell to it, *best* case, by 2016. By the end of 2005, the line hadn't changed; China's import tonnage equaled Canada's <u>entire</u> harvest. The problem will surface before then, but may not be heeded. And closer to home ...

Because of several years of droughts, California had to finally limit water to its farmers. And why should the rest of us care about that?

Because California produces 50% of the
fruit, vegetables and nuts for the entire United States!

Africa now loses over half a million people every month just to starvation. At the end of 2007, the world was losing over 40 million people per year just to starvation ... and the number is growing (And none of this is in our daily media.)

To be "sustainable," a community needs to provide *all* food for its residents. How?

> Agriculture Extension services, usually affiliated with universities, have people – students, faculty, and staff – with interest in sustainable farming, aquaculture, organic foods, etc. They can be helpful in planning and even in staffing, and provide a free service.

> Chinese aquaculture uses sustainable practices that are 5,000 years old. A Chinese group in West Virginia sells fish to New York City buyers. They've volunteered to help.

> The closest to non-oil-based farming seems to be the Amish. In addition to grains, vegetables, fruits, berries, fish, and herbs, we'll need some cows, for dairy and manure; some chickens, for eggs and meat; and some horses, for plowing and manure.

> CSA, Community-Supported Agriculture, may be a key resource for operations. CSA drafted a business plan that includes *all* food provisions they believe is needed for the village. CSA trains biodynamic-based farmers at Wilson College, in Chambersburg, PA.

Referring again to the Barker and Erickson book ...

> *"One pattern of local food growing has become a trend in many parts of the U.S. Farms close to metro areas are inviting families to invest in their harvest. Several hundred families put money up in the spring to finance the planting and harvesting of all sorts of garden vegetables.*

> *"This lowers the cost of financing for the farmer, and guarantees sold products. Some farms require investing families to spend one weekend day per month at the farm."*

> *"An important food technology in this region is the greenhouse. In many climates, local food production can be maintained by using greenhouses."*

Without calling the practice "CSA" ...

Their description is a perfect fit for the pattern that should work to address sustainable quality food provision.

Initial estimates are: a third of an acre, per person, is needed for total food supply. That includes space for root cellars, greenhouses (for longer growing seasons, winter salads, and for starting seeds in winter), small sheltered areas for winter crops, spaces for canning food products, and small structures for growing "fingerling" fish, and other "start-up" animals.

From a physical standpoint, I believe that within a very few years, food will be the biggest sustainability concern ... even in the United States. For example, many people recall that California, suffering from several years of drought, had to limit water available to farmers for the first time in its history. What people don't know:

> California provides 50% of all vegetables, fruits, and nuts for the entire country! We're facing the prospect of having some supermarket shelves empty ... perhaps within two years.

The good news: We do have sufficient arable land with which to provide for our needs ... if we use some of the sustainable systems I've described. Another reference, the Rodale Institute, conducts huge amounts of research into food production – using all healthful organic practices. The technology is there; it's up to us.

The fourth sustainability dimension into which I conducted a lot of research is ...

Leisure

Initially, I considered this to be a kind of "peripheral aspect." Then I discovered it's anything but peripheral. It's another major key to quality-of-life experience.

"Leisure" is defined as anything not part of "work." It can be incredibly pervasive, as most of our lives are spent in leisure times. Plus, leisure probably has the greatest impact on the quality of our lives. Arnold Toynbee had a great quote ...

> *"To be able to fill leisure intelligently*
> *is the last product of civilization."*

I contacted leisure studies specialists, internationally. They *all* knew of Toynbee's quote. But – *none* had anything definitive in response.

A lot of leisure studies look at recreation, and are supported by money from resorts or sports equipment manufacturers. But leisure goes well beyond those arenas. It includes travel, lifelong education, developing special skills, human idea exchange – dialogue – as well as fitness and sports and all the entertainment options.

Pre-Industrial Revolution, the wealthy didn't have to work, and so were known as "the leisure class." We may be at a point in which the needed hours of work are fewer, which can place a multitude of us with a lot of leisure time. The question ...

What's the "stupid" use of leisure?

And what constitutes "filling leisure intelligently"?

In a sense, "leisure" constitutes the largest number of hours of our lives. It goes a lot further than watching a sports event on TV. For example ...

Dr. Richard E. Byrd, a behavioral scientist – and one of my mentors – developed a model by which he could examine the interaction of two behavioral traits that are rarely explored: creativity and risk-taking capacity. He developed a model, "The Creatrix," with a test (which you can find on the Internet.) And he conducted four-day workshops on that model, which intrigued me and which I attended. After everyone had completed a couple of tests, Dr. Byrd offered what I thought was an intriguing definition of risk-taking ...

> *"Think of the hours in a day or week as a pie, and each hour within that duration is a piece of that pie. Then ask who controls the pieces.*
>
> *"When you ask a two-year-old what he or she would like, you'll get a quick response ...'I want this and that and more of it.' Later, however, when you go to school ...*

"Our teacher controls some of those pieces. And our parents now want us to help with chores, so they control some pieces. And we simply have our fun with whatever pieces of time remain.

"Later, when you're married, your spouse wants some pieces, your employer wants some pieces, your kids want some pieces, your friends want some pieces ... and sometimes there aren't many pieces left for you ... to do whatever you want. We can even lose touch with 'I want.'

"When people have too few pieces left just for themselves, they can become depressed. And when you try to reclaim pieces – 'Dear, I know we always go for a walk in the morning, but I have something else I'd like to do.' – we can have guilt trips laid on us. Difficult to reclaim those pieces, once they're lost.

"And the worst part: sometimes when we do have an entire day to just do whatever we'd like, we have a really difficult time thinking of what we'd like most ... what might be most meaningful, for us."

I know it's a lot easier to for me identify what I really don't like than what I do. Dr. Byrd said the biggest aspect of risk-taking was getting in tune with what you really do want and then asking others to honor your needs to do those things.

Now we're talking about real "quality of life" – which is different for each of us, and is truly vital to what I now see as "sustainable living."

This area needs a lot more investigating, so the community can facilitate the best opportunities. It may be an important opportunity never before seen by humanity. A possibility: a "leisure counselor" who listens, helps people discuss and clarify personal preferences and goals ... then crystallize actions to achieve those goals.

Career counselors listen, do some testing, then offer guidance.

Executive coaches listen, do some testing, then provide guidance.

We talk about "lifelong learning," but have no system for making it real.

Leisure, it seems, can be cultural, educational, recreational ... anything we want it to be. And we're at a place in our evolution in which we don't need to work nearly as many hours each week to produce the "food, clothing, and shelter" we all need. Leisure time is growing. It may be one of our most valuable assets. Why not have a skilled professional in the village who can guide us (when we feel the need,) and can help to make the most of our leisure?

And for the fifth dimension in which I did research ...

Transportation

Clustered villages reflect the "New Urbanism" beliefs – replacing driving with walking. The developer of the first New Urbanism project indicated that people readily walk up to ¼ mile. That could accommodate 1,200-2,000 people, depending on density in the village. On-site transport would be walking and bicycling. Moving of goods on site – or people who are not fully ambulatory – would be via electric carts.

For several years, I lived in Georgetown, an historic community within Washington, D.C. I could walk – on lovely brick paved sidewalks, under mature trees – to the vast majority of places I needed to go. Trina and I share one car, and we used it for only about 7,000 miles a year – mostly for Thanksgiving trips to her grandmother's farm in Illinois. And the walking was wonderfully pleasant.

Movement from the site to the larger community can be by car. PV panels could provide sustainable power for a small fleet of electric cars – highway speed with a range of 65 to 120 miles. Barker and Erickson cite another small vehicle ...

> **The Twike**. It's a combination car and bike. Three-wheeled. Uses muscle power with pedals to supplement an electric engine. Goes over 50 mph. Fifty miles per charge; more if you pedal. It's been in Switzerland since 1997 and is a good commuting alternative.

Monitoring column inches of articles, I'm seeing an increasing flow of articles on batteries – with new companies working to make batteries that are lighter, that last longer, and that store more power. I'm also seeing increases in articles concerning photovoltaic power and wind power. All of this almost certainly will lead to the widespread use of all-electric cars in the very near future.

By the way, so-called "hybrid" cars are not really gas-electric. The only external fuel source that goes into them is gas. When we're driving, we have a certain amount of energy. When we brake, we convert that energy to heat. However, the hybrid cars have a device that essentially uses that energy to "wind up" an electric motor, instead of giving off heat. And it clearly gives the car a higher number of miles per gallon. But – it is a gas-powered car. By calling it a gas-electric hybrid, they were able to put many electric car companies out of business.

But the thirst for all-electric cars is growing, and is a momentum I don't see changing. Tesla Motors makes a fantastic, sporty electric car that's fast and has a driving range of about 300 miles. But the Tesla is also very expensive. Looking at a car for the majority of people, several options are emerging ...

> The **REVA** is made in India. It's inexpensive. Top speeds about 50 mph, with 60 - 120 miles per charge, depending on battery type. For now, it's only being distributed in India and a few other countries, but not the United States. One other is now selling overseas ...

The **MDI** is powered by compressed air. Designed by a French scientist and manufactured in India, it's a sedan that has a 300-mile-or-so range, can go highway speeds, and "refills" in seconds – with compressed air from your local service station.

The **Aptera** is an ultra-modern-looking three-wheel, two-passenger electric car with gull-wing doors. It's now available in California, with intent to spread dealerships gradually. You sit at the center of the triangle, making the car very stable. It travels at highway speeds with a range of 120 miles and costs under $27,000.

And the new electric car that should be coming into the United States in 2010 and should be available everywhere ...

The **Leaf**. It's made by Nissan, so will be available all over, at established dealers. It will go 90 mph, has a likely range of 120 miles, is a five-passenger, five-door sedan, and may be quite inexpensive ... targeting a price of only $15,000 ... which I'll believe when I see it.

The **Think** is produced in Norway and sold all over Europe. Ford bought the North American rights to Think. Then, in 2006, Ford sold the rights back to the Norwegians, and the Think – a sporty little 4-passenger sedan that can also go highway speeds and has the usual 120 mile range – should be coming into the U.S. very soon.

The biggest drawback of an electric car is its range and the time required to recharge its batteries. Most require six hours. But – you can often get a 60% charge within an hour or two ... such as by plugging in to a standard residential-type outlet while you're in a meeting or at a restaurant. Generally, 95% of our driving is less than 120 miles a day, so charging it overnight is fairly practical. And if we use photovoltaic panels to generate the power, driving becomes totally sustainable.

To address the slow recharge problem, a company called "Project Better Place" designed a robot that goes under an electric car, removes the depleted batteries, and replaces them with fully charged batteries ...in 45 seconds. They're working with Israel and Denmark to build a large number of robot-operated battery exchange stations, and with Renault, to design a car in which the battery placement is aligned with what the robot does. Then, you simply pull into a station and change batteries in less time – and for a *lot* less money – than it takes to fill a gas tank.

A truck would be needed for bringing goods to the community – or taking surplus food products to a farmers' market. The farm can produce the needed ethanol or biodiesel fuel. Some of the electric car companies also make small truck bodies.

Movement between larger communities will need to be via rail. Rail and light rail are simply the most efficient means of mass transport. However ...

That's probably a huge problem in the United States. It'll likely require a private initiative to connect larger communities, such as using highway rights-of-way for rapid transit. Intermediate speed rail – 100-120 mph – could connect secondary cities, such as a Charlottesville, with major cities, such as D.C., in under two hours. High-speed rail – 180-plus mph – could connect D.C. to Chicago or Atlanta in under four hours. But governments may be reluctant to let go of a system they control. Warren Buffett recently is reputed to have purchased a major railroad, which could signal a shift.

Virtually all highway funds are already used just for maintenance. Increasing fuel prices along with an aging pool of drivers bodes poorly for trucking. Goods will likely shift almost totally to rail transport, with trucks only moving containers regionally, to local distribution centers and to outlet stores. Within a few years, the Interstate highways may be virtually devoid of the traditional convoys of semis.

Air travel seems likely destined only for longer distances, such as over 1,000 miles.

One of the problems explained to me by a "multi-modal transportation" consultant was bureaucratic budgeting. The airport authority has a budget, as does the port authority, and the highway authority, and the rail authority. If you're in an agency, you don't want next year's budget to be less than this year's. However ...

The multi-modal consultant told me that if he were to put in a good rapid-transit system, it would take commuters' cars off the road. Then, some of the planned road widening projects wouldn't be needed. In fact, he said that you could give *free* ridership to people and still save money, overall.

Moving along now to the sixth dimension on which I did research ...

Education

The single most successful form of education – in terms of levels of educational achievement – is home schooling. The movement began mostly with Fundamentalist Christians. It's spread to increasing numbers for non-religious reasons, such as diminishing confidence in public school effectiveness. Quality educational media are already available in a huge range of subjects. The Internet provides far-reaching sources for information. And home schooling lesson plans are available to guide parents. In a sense, "TLC" – with solid support media – seems to do best.

The claim that lack of socialization – not being among a lot of peers – will harm the social growth of children seems to have no supporting evidence. Home-schooled children simply play with others during normal recreational times, and have shown no negative effects, socially. Home schooling is also safer – a growing concern.

Home schooling is also more flexible. Rather than changing subjects or classrooms when the bell rings – a process used to condition us to the "world of work" since the start of the Industrial Revolution – if a student is immersed in a subject and wants to continue for another hour or two ... or three or four ... he or she can do so. Or – if it's a rainy day or a sunny day or a cold day, etc., the school can adjust.

Parents have begun to fatigue, however. Therefore, they are increasingly getting together to home school their children in small groups. One parent takes Monday, one Tuesday, etc. It's still small, personal, and individualized education. And it's less stressful on parents.

The most likely scenario or model seems to be the "one-room schoolhouse" located in the village center – such as at the inn. Home schooling could occur there. And education for <u>all</u> levels, including much of higher education (perhaps in collaboration with online universities) and lifelong learning, would occur there. Lifelong courses could range from advanced degree programs to gourmet cooking, yoga, art, nutrition, literature, philosophy, reading groups ... virtually anything of interest.

The potential for continuing human growth is unprecedented and amazing. I'd guess we've all been through a course about which, when it ended, we thought: *"I'm glad I'm done with that nonsense!"* Looking at the opposite side of things, one of the pioneering leaders of education, John Dewey, defined good education as ...

**An experience that opens new doors ...
and causes a person to want to learn *more*.**

The community will probably need someone – full or part time – to inventory interests and organize quality educational programs for the *entire* community. This could be big ... a mainstay in contributing to leisure and quality-of-life experience.

And that brings us to the seventh dimension on which I did research ...

Trade

I'm definitely not an expert in economics. "Econ 101" was one of my worst under-graduate nightmares. But, from reading I've been doing, I sense that our entire eco-nomic system will likely shift. It probably won't totally collapse, as human needs and the need for trade will always exist. We will all still need services – medical, dental, etc. – and we'll need products, as well. But …

Our system may revert to something like pre-Industrial Revolution economies. The Industrial Revolution gave rise to a large middle class. That class is already diminishing, and polarization – into a greater number of wealthy and poor – is occur-ring … with associated social tensions. (People living on dirt floors watching reruns of *"Baywatch"* begin to feel frustration and anger … which can lead to terrorism.)

In addition to oil, another motivation for the Iraq invasion was protection of the pet-rodollar. Iran and Iraq were negotiating with France and Germany to trade oil in Euros. The petrodollar has been a global standard for a long time. Confidence in the dollar is one of the underpinnings of our economy. Personal trade is readily ac-complished using international currency: VISA or AmEx. But they need a base for currency exchange. A shift from the dollar to another currency (such as the Euro, Yen, or Yuan) as a standard would be disastrous for the U.S. economy.

India and China are experiencing tremendous surges in economic growth, based largely on providing cheap labor for manufacturing. India is also provid-ing more skilled services, such as operating call centers for product distributors or writing new software for Microsoft and others. However, both countries suffer from …

- Water depletion;

- Extreme environmental degradation;

- And a strain on their ability to provide food for their populations.

According to WorldWatch Institute …

> *"If not reversed, environmental deterioration threatens to become a ma-jor impediment to the economic development of China and India."*

> *"As China and India add their surging consumption to that of the United States, Europe, and Japan, the most important question is this: Can the world's ecosystems withstand the damage – the increase in carbon emissions, the loss of forests, the extinction of species – that are now in prospect?"*

And …

"The rise of China and India is the wake-up call that should prompt the people in the United States and around the world to take seriously the need for strong commitments to build sustainable economies."

Dr. David Martin, a global economic adviser, described pacts, known as Basel-1 and Basel-2, that facilitate international banking movement, to which banking systems have agreed. They went into effect on January 1, 2008. Dr. Martin finds no evidence that any U.S. bank was even close to compliance. The result could be a shift by countries, such as China, and multinational corporations to begin banking in other countries and currencies. If this happens, Dr. Martin indicated that confidence in the dollar could plummet, and the U.S. economy could take a major hit.

How do we deal with global economic instability?

One approach is to look at a sustainable village as a self-contained entity – as it is with regard to power, water, etc. Then, the system would have two parts ...

1. Someone would need to examine all the needs the community has ... garden maintenance, farming, food canning, geothermal equipment maintenance, operating the educational system, serving in a coffee shop, leisure coaching, etc. For each task, estimate the amount of time needed, and when that time is needed, (as harvesting will likely demand more time at some times of the year than others, and a coffee shop might be busier at some times than others.)

2. Someone may need to serve as a personal growth coach for each resident. He or she would help the resident identify his or her biggest interests and growth needs. If interests correspond to a need the community has, a match is made. If interests don't – such as painting or writing or meditating – that's still OK. Often, people can kick in a part of their time to help satisfy a community need – even though it clearly doesn't support their personal growth needs.

    Or they can use cash or something like a barter system to compensate for (for example) the food they're receiving from the community.

Using a personal growth coach this way also could have a major positive impact on *"the intelligent use of leisure,"* on lifelong education, and quality-of-life feelings.

Next, how will "widget manufacturing" occur?

Each sustainable community will need some commodities – from computers to toilet paper – to satisfy the needs of residents. Some thoughts from *Going Local* ...

"Johan Galtung, a leading peace theorist from Norway, elaborates the rationale for communities to become self-reliant ...

"Produce what you need using your own resources, internalizing the challenges this involves, growing with the challenges, neither giving the most challenging tasks (positive externalities) to somebody else on whom you become dependent, nor exporting negative externalities to somebody else to whom you do damage and who may become dependent on you.

"... The justification for doing so is clear: we will enjoy the positive externalities, rather than giving them away, and at the same time will be responsible ourselves for the negative externalities ... We can fight the negative consequences ourselves, the distance between cause and effect being a short one."

Continuing with additional thoughts from *Going Local* ...

"A community can – indeed, must – maintain economic relationships with the rest of the world, provided it retains control of these relationships. Three categories can help accomplish this:

"The first is to nurture businesses that reduce imports for basic needs. A sound local economy is one that provides everyone with the necessities of life, and trades surplus production for less-essential goods and services.

"The second is to keep ownership of business local, so that the sudden departure of a firm on which the community depends is virtually impossible.

"The third strategy is to channel local savings and investment capital into the building of the local economy.

"A community committed to import substitution, however, aims to minimize population growth. The goal is to expand the quantity and quality of jobs without drawing new people. Where jobs grew fastest, family income grew more slowly than the national average. Where employment growth was slowest, income growth was above the national average.

"People with rising incomes tend to buy goods featuring higher levels of technology, such as VCRs, personal computers, software, and medical instruments. The delinking of production from bulk materials diminishes the importance of locating a factory near natural resources.

"And this opens up more opportunities for community corporations almost anywhere to produce a greater variety of goods.

"Services requiring a high degree of human skill, which are becoming a larger and larger fraction of the nation's economy ...

... will necessarily remain local.

"If services, knowledge, and technology are substituting for materials, it follows that the most competitive communities will be those that are smartest, not largest.

"Of the 90,000 manufacturing companies in the Emilia-Romagna region (of Italy), 97 percent employ fewer than 50 employees. A network typically forms temporarily to create a specific product for a well-defined niche market. Participating firms pool their resources and share the risk. Once the project is complete, the network disbands. Following successful models in Europe, more than 50 flexible manufacturing networks have been set up in the United States."

This trend opens new opportunities for decentralized production ...

"The increasing capability to span boundaries and borders that networking affords to business would seem to have tilted the playing field decisively against locally elected and appointed economic development planners vis-à-vis the plant location managers of the multinational companies at the hubs or apexes of the network.

"Yet at the same time, precisely because the networking principle allows concentrated business organizations to coordinate operations across an ever more dispersed field of play, more decentralized production becomes increasingly feasible."

"Therefore, a critical feature of a needs driven economy is local ownership. The relatively small size of CSAs, ESCOs, WASCOs, and recycling makes local ownership not only possible but also probable. And for complex goods and services that can be produced only on a larger economy of scale ... networks of locally owned businesses – whether clustered in one community or spread out globally – can do the job.

"The key to transforming the local economy was not to combat business but to remake it. Today, more then 1,500 cooperatives in the Emilia-Romagna region employ 60,000 workers. Many of these small businesses export high-tech products that compete internationally. Creatively blending public-private partnerships with worker ownership transformed a once-impoverished agricultural area into the fastest growing part of Italy, with the tenth highest per capita income among the 122 official regions of the European Community."

One other concern expressed by people concerned over the instability of the dollar centers around identifying a more stable means of exchange. Bartering has grown for decades, largely as a means of tax avoidance. It's more widespread than most people know, and is growing. Exchange groups have already worked out ways to ...

... equate tomatoes with dental services. *Going Local* goes further...

> *"Today, hundreds of communities worldwide print their own currencies to induce residents to pump up their local economies. A community currency, whether in the form of coins, paper bills, checks, or computer-tallied credits and debits, is essentially a system to promote local purchasing. The managers of the system decide which goods and services qualify for exchange, and exactly what residents need to do to join. With the time-consuming tasks of screening already performed, consumers and producers know that any purchase or sale within the money system helps the local economy.*

> *"The Local Exchange Trading System – LETS – uses a simple computer program and a currency called "green money." Residents barter different goods and services with one another, and report the transactions. Each person's account has credits and debits posted.*

> *"LETS is both self-propelling and self-regulating. It's self-propelling because individuals whose accounts are in surplus have an incentive to go out and strike deals with others in the community. It's self-regulating because anyone can log onto the computer system, see anyone else's tally, and decide not to do business with a person whose account was too deep in the hole. Most operating LETS place a limit on indebtedness.*

> *"One of the shortcomings of LETS is they tend to involve individual craftsmen and service providers, not large businesses. The first one had 500 participants, but only 5 were shops, all small. The key is ensuring that real needs, as opposed to peripheral pleasures, can be met through a LETS."*

Finally ... one additional source of information about trade, about money and currency systems, and – more important – about how they impact sustainability. These incredibly detailed yet wonderfully expansive thoughts, essentially about "commerce and life," come from *"The Future of Money,"* by Bernard Lietaer.

The following public "Warning to Humanity" was unanimously agreed upon by 1,600 scientists, including a majority of living Nobel Prize winners in the sciences:

> *"A great change in stewardship of the Earth and the life on it is required, if vast human misery is to be avoided and our global home on this planet is not be irretrievably mutilated ... If not checked, many of our current practices may so put at serious risk the future that we wish for human society and the plant and animal kingdoms, and may so alter the living world, that it will be unable to sustain life in the manner that we know. Fundamental changes are urgent if we are to avoid the collision our present course will bring about."* Therefore ...

Unless precautions are taken, there is a 50-50 chance that the next five to ten years will see a dollar crisis amounting to a global money meltdown. Aspects of our monetary system that met the objectives of another age, the Industrial Revolution, are inadequate for the challenges facing us in an Information Age. In fact ...

Working solutions are under way. Thousands of communities, globally, have their own money initiatives. They create new wealth, while solving social problems without taxation or regulation. They are empowering self-organizing communities, while increasing overall economic and social stability. And ...

They enable the creation of essential *social capital*.

Money has the potential to contribute to global abundance, sustainability, and peace of mind if used wisely; when restricted in its flow, it also has the ability to engender unfathomable suffering and hardship.

Using different currency types results in different social outcomes. Some money systems foster cooperation; others competition. 1/3 to 1/2 of conventional monetary functions will be picked up by new currencies. Result: recession and unemployment severity are significantly reduced. Being aware of their effects, we can choose among these currencies when making different financial transactions. Beyond the standard federally sanctioned currencies, many options exist.

A fourth of global trade uses barter – no currency at all. Barter has existed since the dawn of mankind, so it is often seen as an "inferior" or "primitive" form of exchange, sometimes associated with the underground economy. This has totally changed over the past decades. Barter even has two major trade organizations ...

The International Reciprocal Trade Association And, The Corporate Barter Council.

Another manner of exchange is "complementary currency." This constitutes an agreement among a group of people or corporations to accept non-traditional currency as an exchange medium. They're "complementary" because they don't replace conventional national currency but perform social functions that official currency is not designed to handle.

In January 2000, over 2,500 complementary currency systems operated in over a dozen countries; 400 in the UK alone. These currencies are emerging money revolution prototypes. The future of money lies with both further computerization of conventional currencies – such as dollars, euros or yen via smart cards and other new technologies – *and* with mainstreaming of complementary currencies.

Our ability to make knowledgeable choices in money systems allows us to imagine, devise, and support different futures.

In a traditional money system, the application of interest has three outcomes ...

1. Interest indirectly encourages systematic competition among the participants in the system.

2. Interest continually fuels the need for endless economic growth, even when actual standards of living remain stagnant.

3. Interest concentrates wealth by taxing the vast majority in favor of a small minority.

What is "natural" – competition or cooperation?

Kyoto University professor Imanishi showed Darwin's vision of nature as a struggle for life to be blind to co-evolution, symbiosis, joint development, and harmonious coexistence that prevail in all domains of evolution. Our bodies would not survive without the symbiotic collaboration of billions of digestive tract microorganisms.

Evolutionary biologist Elisabet Sahtouris shows that predominantly competitive behavior is a characteristic of a young species during its first forays in the world. In contrast, in mature systems (e.g., an old-growth forest,) the competition for light is balanced by intense cooperation among species. Species that do not learn to cooperate with the species with which they are codependent, invariably disappear.

Interest causes a systemic transfer of wealth from the bottom 80% of the population to the top 10%. This transfer is due exclusively to the monetary system in use, and is completely independent of the degree of cleverness or industriousness of the participants, the classic argument to justify large income differences. In the US, the top 1% now has more personal wealth than the bottom 92% combined.

The most powerful catalyst of the Information Age transformation is not information, but the *communication* revolution. Information tends to leak. The more it leaks, the more we have, and the more of us have it. Government classifications, trade secrecy, intellectual property rights, and confidentiality are all attempts at artificially reducing this natural tendency to leak. Artificial attempts fail because the conduits of their delivery system can be owned, not the actual information.

Information expands as it is used. Information spontaneously tends towards abundance, not scarcity. In a way, this is a drawback: we all complain of information overload. What remains scarce and competitive is human attention – our ability to understand, turn into knowledge, and *use* all the information available to us.

The switch to information-as-a-resource means that governments are less able to intervene in the high-speed train of social transformation that is headed our way. Information is more *accessible* to more people than the world's key resources have ever been before. In the nature of *things,* the "few" had access to key resources; the "many" did not. Information-as-resource encourages ...

- Spreading benefits rather than concentrating wealth; information can be more readily shared than petroleum, gold, or even water.

- Maximizing choice rather than suppressing diversity; the informed are harder to regiment than the uninformed.

Key differences between the concepts of data, information, knowledge, and wisdom:

Data are undigested observations without context. A list of phone numbers is an example of raw data.

Information is data organized according to some system aimed at making it retrievable and useful. An alphabetical listing in a phone book organizes phone number raw data in such a usable way.

Knowledge is information you've internalized, integrated into everything else you know from experience and study, and have available as a basis for action in your life. You know a particular phone number is your friend's number; this links with everything else you know about that friend. An increasingly important form of knowledge is learning *how* to find the information that's useful to you.

Wisdom adds depth, perspective, and meaning to knowledge by integrating ways of knowing other than logic and analysis, such as intuition, intelligence, or compassion of the heart. It's multi-dimen-sional, crossing boundaries between different fields of knowledge. It's an ultimate synthesis; it can't be forced on or taught to someone else:

"We can be knowledgeable with other people's knowledge, but we cannot be wise with other people's wisdom."

Michel de Montaigne

What matters most is not the technology, but *the way we use it.* The whole money game is going to change. Additional choices beyond national currencies are both unavoidable and necessary. The starting point is to be aware that choice in money systems exists, and that choice matters.

From Bernard Lietaer's *The Future of Money,* come four pictures of "plausible futures" to consider. Each scenario gives rise to very different possible directions in which changes in our money system could take us ...

Scenario #1: "The Corporate Millennium"

- Of the 100 richest economies, 51 are corporations. E.g., sales by General Motors have been greater than Denmark's GDP, or Ford's than South Africa.

- The world's two hundred largest corporations now control 28% of the global economy, yet need to employ only 0.3% of its population to achieve that.

- The sales of the world's largest two hundred corporations are equivalent to 30% of global domestic product. Their total annual sales are larger than the combined GDP of 182 countries – all but the largest nine countries.

- About one-third of global trade is really intra-corporate trade, i.e., one subsidiary exporting to another subsidiary controlled by the same corporation.

- U.S. corporations pay fewer taxes than they receive in taxpayer subsidies.

- In 1997, *Business Week* reported that average compensation for CEOs of these publicly subsidized corporations soared to $5.5 million a year; wages of the working population were stagnant. In the 1960s, CEO salaries were 30x greater than those of the average worker, compared with 200x today.

- For every dollar in total taxes (local, state, federal) paid by individuals, corporations used to pay seventy-six cents in the early 1950s. By 1980-92, corporate taxes were down to twenty-one cents per dollar of personal taxes.

Mainstream media aims not so much to inform or report, as to shape public opinion in accordance with agendas of prevailing corporate powers. As Lietaer states ...

> *"Virtually everywhere the mass media provide people primarily with commercial messages. It is hard to discover in most of today's news media the kind of information that would help citizens of democratic societies reach well-informed political decisions. The media have been called 'Weapons of Mass Distraction.' "*

It is almost as though we were being invaded by alien beings intent on colonizing the planet, reducing us to serfs, then excluding as many of us as possible. And ...

> *"The main problem of the future will be the glut of unnecessary people who will be irrelevant to the needs of corporations, and therefore will be uneducated, untrained, ageing and resentful...The slow redistribution of wealth to which we became accustomed after World War II is already rapidly reversed, so the future is one of inequality. We are entering an age of hopelessness, an age of resentment, an age of rage...The world belongs to the global corporation. The nation state is desperately sick."*

Next ...

Scenario #2: "Careful Communities"

It's a modern version of Western Europe in the centuries after the Roman Empire collapse. It's a return to small-scale, homogeneous communities, fragmented by vast forests. Each has its own currency, administration, and inbred worldviews.

The "Big Monetary Crash" will occur when the U.S. dollar comes under attack.

It is not a question of whether, but only a question of *when*.

The instabilities of the official monetary system will assail that linchpin currency of the global money system. People will have to reorganize their lives to be more local and self-sustaining, and use different forms of governance. Control over local currencies can be used to lock people into a safety cocoon. Local currencies can be used positively or negatively.

In the "Careful Community" scenario, their restrictive potential is revealed.

Scenario #3: "Hell on Earth"

Instead of people organizing into self-contained communities, an individualistic free-for-all ensues. It is the world that results if enough people believe that the solution to any breakdown is to buy more bullets for their guns ... *Mad Max*.

Scenario #4: "Sustainable Abundance"

It is ironic that only monks who don't own anything – or possibly the very rich or the extraordinarily gifted – can afford equanimity about money. The rest of us, the vast majority – even in the richest countries – succumb to the obligation of "making a living" that does not really coincide with what we'd *like* to be doing or being.

> How much do we give up of our being,
> of who we really want to be,
> in making a living?

Many do not dare to find out what they'd really like to do, out of fear that it would be too painful to go back to a "normal" job after that. The game we play is that when we retire – and have put enough money aside – then we will take care of our dreams. Some take it in little installments; we rush through a week, looking forward to the weekend or a vacation, when we will do what we really want to do.

Now, why are we exploring these scenarios?

These scenarios present options.

> *"If this happens in the world, then this is likely to happen ... which means that these other events are likely to occur ... so we should ..."*

They help us plan the consequences of our choices. They are tools used in the broad category of "strategic planning."

How do currency choices affect conditions such as sustainability?

One definition, taught to campers arriving at a campsite ...

> **"Leave the place in better shape than you found it.**
>
> **And you have no assurance that anyone will ever use this campsite again."**

"Abundance" is what provides enough freedom of choice in the material domain to as many people as possible, so they can express their passion and creativity. Such creativity is the expression of their highest form of consciousness ... their highest calling ... and it provides a sense of meaning in their life.

To realize the benefits of an information society, the transition will require *both* knowledge and wisdom. If we opt to have wisdom prevail, the Information Revolution could help us create "Sustainable Abundance," rather than other scenarios.

> Would you continue doing what you are doing if you had all the money you would ever need?

If the answer is yes, you're among the fortunate ones whose work and job coincide.

Evidence indicates jobs without meaning can make you sick and even kill you.

> *"If the economic problem (the struggle for subsistence) is solved, mankind will be deprived of its traditional purpose...*
>
> *"Thus for the first time since his creation man will be faced by his real, his permanent problem...*
>
> *"There is no country and no people. I think, who can look forward to the age of leisure and abundance without a dread. It is a fearful problem for the ordinary person, with no special talents occupy himself, especially if he no longer has roots to the soil or in custom or in the beloved conventions of a traditional society."*
>
> John Maynard Keynes

If Keynes is right ...

For the first time in history we'll be forced to reinvent ourselves, to find other ways to identify who we are. We'll no longer identify with "professional labels." We'll need other identities, other reasons, that give purpose to our lives. There's enough work to be done in your community to keep everyone busy for the rest of his or her life. Work can express our unique creativity. The question is ...

Have we become so hypnotized by our fear of money scarcity that we also fear lack of work?

Most people will be involved part time in both economies. Within a family, some members may be employed mostly in the global competitive economic loop, while others might be active mostly in the local economy. Both might be "following their bliss," ideally both having the opportunity for their ideal work also to be their job.

> *Such an outcome is possible within an "integral economy," which consists of the traditional, competitive economy on one side, and a local, cooperative economy on the other. The former produces financial capital, and the latter, social capital. They can operate in symbiosis with each other.*

What's most surprising is how close we were to such a solution in the 1930s. However, governments did not give this approach a chance. They stopped it because it worked *too* well without the need for central government involvement. Here are some examples of successful complementary currency systems ...

Stamp scrip was applied in **Worgl,** Austria, population 4,500, with 500 jobless people, and another 1,000 in the immediate vicinity. 200 families were penniless. The mayor placed 40,000 Austrian schillings in a bank – a pittance compared to what needed to be done to improve the city – then issued 40,000 schillings' worth of stamp scrip. He used the stamp scrip to pay for his first project.

As a stamp was applied each month (at 1% of face value), everybody paid with the stamp scrip was sure to spend it quickly, providing work for others. When people ran out of ideas of what to spend their stamp scrip on, they paid their taxes early.

Worgl repaved streets, rebuilt the water system, and completed all the projects on the mayor's list. The town built new houses, a ski jump, and a bridge. The bulk of the work was provided by the circulation of the stamp scrip *after* the first people contracted by the mayor spent it. In fact, each schilling of stamp scrip created 12 to 14 times more employment than the normal schillings circulating in parallel.

Worgl's demonstration was so successful, it was replicated in 200 Austrian townships. Then the central bank panicked and asserted its monopoly rights. It became a criminal offense in Austria to issue "emergency currency." Worgl returned to 30% unemployment. Widespread social unrest exploded throughout Austria.

And unrest often leads to the emergence of a "savior." In this case ...

Hitler. The rest is history.

Stamping out popular grass-roots initiatives, where people try to solve their problems locally, pushed a sophisticated and educated society into violently suppressing its minorities, towards less and less democracy and, ultimately, towards war.

WIR is a Swiss complementary currency run by a community of individuals and small business people. It is the oldest continuous system in the modern Western world, founded in 1934 by 16 members in Zurich. It has continuously grown in both participant numbers and business volume. It proves complementary currencies make sense, even in a conservative, hard-nosed, capitalist country with one of the world's highest living standards. By 1994, WIR grew to 2.5 billion Swiss francs annual volume (over $2 billion) with 80,000 members from all over the country.

The Local Exchange Trading System, **LETS,** the most frequently used complementary currency system, was invented in the 1980s by Michael Linton, in British Columbia, Canada. It uses a local non-profit corporation as a mutual credit company. The only actual asset is the personal computer for record keeping. You pay a small set-up fee and an annual membership fee, to cover record-keeping costs.

Electronic or physical notice boards indicate someone offering a specific service. If you buy it, your account is debited; the seller's is credited. The amount is negotiated, and can combine "green dollars" and national currency. Participants handle the cash. Green dollar exchanges are phoned in or sent by note or e-mail. All participants can see all accounts, so no one's likely to hoard or overspend. In 2000, Canada had 25-30 LETS operating, more in the UK, and it's quickly spreading.

In **Time Dollars,** begun by Professor Edgar S. Cahn in Washington, D.C., someone gets an hour of credit for an hour of help. That hour – recorded on a computer or manual system – can be spent buying goods or services elsewhere. As one gets a credit, another gets a debit, so the sum of all Time Dollars in the system is always zero. And everyone gets the help or goods he wants.

> Retirement homes using Time Dollars found that the money knit the group together. People say hello to each other, celebrate birthdays, look out for each other, and do things as a community, such as having a community garden. This simple device changes the way people relate to each other.

> People feel that their contributions are rewarded. They feel valued. One unexpected side effect: Participants got healthier!

> To encourage its use, a Brooklyn, New York health insurance company, Elderplan, accepts 25% of the premiums for its senior health programs in Time Dollars.

Ithaca HOURS were set at $10, the average hourly wage in the area. They issue physical currency in different denominations. And ...

They publish a bi-monthly newspaper that advertises the products and services of people and businesses that accept Ithaca HOURS. The paper typically includes about 1,200 listings, including over 200 businesses. Advertisers can provide quotes in both currencies, e.g., $10 per hour, 60% in Ithaca HOURS, 40% in U.S. dollar currency. (Paul Glover has a $25 kit describing how to set up the system.) 39 HOURS systems were operating in 2000.

The system is workable. The risk: the Ithaca Reserve Board has to decide how much currency to issue – or it could experience inflation. It also develops hour variances – e.g., an hour of a house painter versus an hour of a neurosurgeon.

Tlaloc, begun in Mexico and named for an Aztec rain god, is a mutual credit system in which the currency is issued in the form of paper checks. The checks have endorsement spaces on the back, so the first user can endorse it for the next user, and so on. The last endorser brings the check to the center, where the last user is credited and initial issuer is debited. The system, therefore, has both mutual credit and paper currency. It requires only a personal computer to keep accounts.

Some complementary currencies are local loyalty schemes, aimed at creating local employment; small businesses will be the major source of future employment. They make sense socially, economically, and from a business viewpoint. Findings:

- Complementary currencies make possible transactions and exchanges that otherwise would not occur. This means in practice that more economic activity – implying more work and wealth – is being created than would otherwise be the case.

- Additional work and wealth are being generated where they are needed most, without need for taxes or government bureaucracy, and without creating risk of inflation in the mainstream economy.

- Small businesses can easily accept the currency, because they can spend it in the community, e.g., farmers using local harvest labor.

World over, we hear the same complaint …

"Things aren't the way they used to be.
We used to have a better sense of community."

Consequences include vandalism against common property and criminality, particularly in the younger generation. The U.S. social identity median has moved from the nuclear family to the single-parent family; 51% of all U.S. children live in a single-parent home. In a recent survey of the priorities of the American population, the desire to "rebuild neighborhoods and communities" received the highest ranking for an astounding 86% of the population.

Anthropologists have found …

A sense of community is based on *reciprocity in gift exchanges.*

A commercial transaction is a closed system; you buy a box of nails from a hardware store and give it money. However, if a neighbor happens to have extra nails and gives them to you, that leaves an imbalance in the transaction that some possible future transaction completes ... such as asking you for a cup of sugar. A gift transaction creates something that the monetary exchange does not. A new thread has been woven into the community fabric. From the Latin ...

> *Cum* means *together, among each other.*
> *Munus* means *gift*, or the verb *munere*, to give.

Hence "community" equals *"to give among each other."* In Japan, gifts often take the form of sharing one's talents in art, calligraphy, culture, or other social graces.

It is not the monetary value of the gift that matters; what counts is the *intention*, the quality of the personal touch.

To unravel the community fabric, do the opposite of what created it. Communities break down when non-reciprocal monetary exchanges replace gift exchanges.

Governments support complementary currency systems at three levels of effort ...

1. **"Passive tolerance"** is most common. *"It doesn't break any laws, so let it be."*

2. **"Mildly supportive"** – as in New Zealand and the U.S. – has local governments funding and helping to organize complementary currency start-ups. Adding more police is proven, time and again, to not reduce crime. Throwing money at failing education does not remedy the problem. Nothing can replace a community where people watch out for each other, or where older children mentor younger ones.

3. **"Strongly supportive"** involves systematic funding for complementary currency initiatives that provide better social results at a lower governmental cost. The Japanese government is completely funding eco-currency activities, and is considering paying for the accounting and clearing systems for Healthcare Time Accounts.

The hard part of creating currency is not conceiving a new variation of complementary currency, nor even starting it. The hard part is having it accepted and used in a community. As for all currencies, what is most needed is credibility – without it, nothing will happen. The most important factor to start a local currency is local leadership. Someone, or some group, needs vision, entrepreneurial capability, and charisma. The best leadership is when, at the end ...

People claim they did it themselves.

If a local currency does not tie into the national one, the unit that makes the most sense is the hour. The hour is a universal standard, and almost all contemporary systems which do not tie their unit to the national currency are using it.

Two important reasons why a mutual credit system (backed by some commodity standard, such as gold,) is preferable to a fiat system, (backed by pure trust,) particularly for systems designed to be scaled up or replicated in large numbers:

1. The amount of currency remains the same. As people engage in transactions in the opposite direction of their initial trade (e.g., someone who had a credit in one transaction, and uses the credit to purchase a good or service brings his or her balance back to zero.) This self-regulating feature is important, because it eliminates the most tricky and treacherous decision in currency management.

2. The second reason is strategic. Mutual credit complementary currencies do not pose such a threat, and therefore could grow in importance in time without interfering with central bank duties.

Historian Arnold Toynbee found two causes for the collapse of 21 past civilizations:

1. Extreme concentration of wealth; and ...

2. Inflexibility in the face of changing conditions.

Only three methods have been identified for persuading people to engage in non-spontaneous behavior change ...

1. Education and moral persuasion;

2. Financial interest; and ...

3. Regulation

History shows whenever financial interests contradict regulations, financial interests usually end up the winners. When financial interests run up against moral pressure, the battle is often more difficult. Many people decide they either cannot afford, or do not care enough, to follow moral advice when it costs them something.

A 20th century pioneer, Duane Elgin, claims that humanity has always been at its best when its capacities are challenged to the maximum. We either radically and consciously change toward sustainability, in all regards, or we disappear like the dinosaurs did before us. The secret of the current shift is a succession of three waves, which overlapped in time around the turn of the century ...

1. A **Value-Shift Wave** in which the old modernist values were gradually commuted into the values of the Age of Integration;

2. The **Information Wave**, which enabled unprecedented access to knowledge for vast numbers of people; and ...

3. The **Money Wave**, whereby new money systems complemented the old national currency system.

In the 1990s most people were only aware of the Information Wave. The media focused on it. In reality, all three mutations were already well on their way if we looked beyond the reports from officialdom.

A continuously evolving money system operates simultaneously on different levels, from global to local. The advantage of a multiple-level money system is ...

Each activity is supported by the currency best adapted to the circumstance.

Convertibility among the different currencies is ensured on the Net whenever that is needed. The following table sets out the criteria for classifying the different currency types.

	Yang	Yin
Effects on Relationships	Scarce/ Competition-inducing	Sufficient/ Cooperation-promoting
Manner of Creation	"Fiat," created by a central authority	"Mutual credit," created by the participants themselves

Social capital is best nurtured by cooperation-inducing yin currencies, while global industrial trade would be best handled by competition-generating yang currencies.

Different currency types tend to induce different kinds of relationships among users. Where you want a cooperative, egalitarian type of relationship, use yin type currencies. They build social capital. In contrast, trading with yang currencies will tend to shape competitive hierarchical relationships, perfectly appropriate for certain business contexts. They build financial capital.

Awareness of the need for "social capital" in a healthy society is growing. Cooperative currencies are simply a tool to foster it. In the yang cycle, financial capital is fostered. The yin cycle nurtures and develops social capital. Both types of capital – financial and social – are indispensable for human activity to flourish.

The goal of an integral economy is to create integral wealth. This is developed when all four types of capital – natural, social, financial, and physical – are in balance. By confusing wealth with only financial capital ...

We risk believing we can deplete our natural or social capital indefinitely. Below a certain level of natural or social capital, financial capital no longer has relevance.

A huge bank account in a wasteland of social disorder or ecological collapse is meaningless and worthless.

To achieve integral economy balance, four levels of currency are essential:

1.   A global reference currency

2.   Three main multinational currencies

3.   Some national currencies

4.   Local complementary currencies

Two sustainability studies – *"Beyond the Limits"* and the Global Business Network's *"Sustainability"* – showed that *both* value shifts and technological shifts are needed concurrently. After evaluating and modeling the relationships between global resources, population, industrial output, and pollution, the authors concluded ...

> *"The potential for technological innovations only buys time – there is still a collapse, but it is delayed until the middle of the 21st century. Radical behavioral and attitudinal changes are explored too, but it turns out that these alone are not enough either – there is still a crash in the mid-21st century. It is only when both these kinds of changes are applied together that a crash is avoided."*

Best I can tell, this combination *is* happening. It's an historically extraordinary shift in values in less than one generation. The "cultural creative" subculture is leading this value-shift wave. The two types of cultural creatives are ...

- "Green" cultural creatives (13% or 21 million in the U.S,) are concerned with environment and social concerns from a secular viewpoint. They tend to be public arena activists. They focus on solving problems "out there" and are less interested in personal change.

- "Core" cultural creatives (10.6% or 20 million) have personal evolution and green values. They are engaged in psychology, spiritual life, self-actualization, self-expression. They enjoy mastering new ideas and are concerned with social and ecological sustainability.

Another Duane Elgin study indicates that this shift is also happening globally ...

> *"Considered together, trends seem to indicate that a global paradigm shift is underway."*

The global population at large is everywhere ahead in the transition compared to both their official leaders and their media. The problem ...

Modernist opinion leaders, separately, often dismiss each of these trends as a "quirk" or an insignificant "fashion." However, when considered together, the pattern reveals a major shift towards yin values in all aspects of society. The pattern includes disparate concerns about ...

- the environment;
- chaos theory in physics;
- holistic health care practices;
- the women's emancipation movement;
- bridging the Cartesian split between matter and spirit;
- networks replacing hierarchical structures (Net & Virtual Organizations).

As a caterpillar evolves into a butterfly, civilization is in the dissolution phase:

> Imaginal cells use cybersphere to interconnect
> outside traditional communication channels.

Sustainable Abundance, as the butterfly, is an available outcome.

When I began exploring "trade" or "commerce," I had no idea how involved it would get, or how relevant it would be to sustainability. But – this thinking provides an opportunity for residents in a sustainable village to flourish – regardless of what might happen to the dollar or to national or international economies.

And – I especially like and value the link between exchange currencies and social capital. The right currency evidently improves social capital ... which improves quality-of-life feelings ... which improves overall happiness ... which encourages me to make a sustainable village a physical reality.

And for the eighth dimension, we have ...

The Internet

Somehow, it will likely still be with us ... though it may evolve with better and better features. English seems to be the language of the world, boosted largely by computers and the Internet. It's the second language in India, China, most of Europe, and even in little Himalayan countries such as Nepal or Bhutan. There is a global feeling that to be part of the modern world, you need to know English. The Internet enables us to secure data and commodities from anywhere ...

- In addition to research data, a huge number of international newspapers and other information periodicals are available on-line, free.

- We can travel anywhere, as virtually all transportation and lodging is available on the Internet, using credit cards for reservations.

- We can buy products from anywhere, and have them come to us via any number of carriers. And ...

- We can very easily and inexpensively communicate with people all over the world – in writing (with e-mails and even lengthy attachments,) by voice (Internet phones,) by video (e.g., Skype,) and by social networking (e.g., Facebook and Twitter.)

The Internet is melting national boundaries – which creates headaches for governments looking to collect taxes, or control information. But it seems to be an irreversible direction. As civilization sustains and continues, future communities will likely be "connected," hence, we have reinforcement of an earlier quote ...

"Think globally, but live locally."

And for the ninth dimension in which I did research ...

Infrastructure

This dimension concerns power, water, wastewater collection and treatment, solid waste management, recycling, etc. ... the enabling physical environment. After World War II, we moved towards large, centralized systems, such as nuclear power plants that could serve an entire region. Now, trends in all aspects of infrastructure have been moving towards smaller, more decentralized systems.

Equipment should be readily available to support smaller systems. However, the issue is not just generation; storage is often the bigger issue ...

- A clear day with PV panels generates plenty of power – but someone does laundry in the evening, watches TV at night, etc.

- It's windy all night, but everyone's asleep; not much power needed.

- It rains all night ... as everyone's asleep. Then, in the morning, everyone needs water for bathing and cooking.

Power is readily created. Stanford completed a survey of over 8,000 sites around the world, to determine the potential for wind power. It found the world has more than enough ability to satisfy *all* power needs with wind alone, including room for growth. It's also reputed to be the least expensive form of power generation ... when nuclear includes the cost to produce the rods and dispose of waste.

Projections that "alternative sources" might contribute 3% or 5% have no foundation in fact, whatever. Some northern European countries are already generating half or more of all their power with wind machines.

From seeing a steadily increasing number of column inches on wind power and photovoltaic power, and seeing those modes having double-digit rates of growth, year after year, I expect a huge and continuing rate of growth.

- When Warren Buffet announced he was planning multiple wind farms across Iowa, many were surprised.

- When T. Boone Pickens announced he was investing billions in wind farms near his ranch in Texas, people sat back ... but were a little less surprised.

- And when you see wind machines on hilltops as you drive along highways, it's noticeable, but less shocking.

I don't think wind power is at the bottom of the bell curve any longer. It seems to be clearly moving up and into the mainstream of acceptance. And for the other primary "alternative source" ...

Photovoltaic panels are dropping in price per amount of power provided. The panels are now backlogged almost five months, suggesting public concern for increasing oil prices ... and for "being green." Even "Harry Homeowner" can contemplate adding PV panels to his roof; they're affordable and are applicable at smaller scale than the giant wind machines.

The panels are also becoming more and more efficient. And they still have a huge rate of growth. (Most growth is in Japan, then in Europe, however.)

The biggest problem in power, however, is ...

Storage. People need the power "whenever." Pittsburgh, for example, generates huge amounts of hydropower. But – the amount of power is the same, hour after hour, while demand fluctuates. The city uses excess power – such as exists during the night – to pump water to a reservoir. As demand increases in the morning, and the city needs more power than it's generating, it releases water through turbines. It's a good way to match supply with demand. But ...

Small developments, villages, or communities can't build giant reservoirs – especially if they lie in a fairly flat region. So ...

How do we enjoy power availability
when the sun's down and there's no wind?

Batteries work, but are questionable as a long-term solution. They're expensive, have a five to ten year life, use some toxic materials, and may not be as available, long term. They're likely better for cars than for entire communities. However ...

A new company is completing design of a battery that handles the loads for an entire home. It's the size of a refrigerator, and can be located in a corner of the garage. Charge the battery with PV panels and have sufficient power for all of your home needs, at all times. Homes – and the village – could disconnect from the grid.

Hydrogen fuel cells have been touted as the savior source; they're really a means of storage, not a "source" of power. One of the basic laws of physics is:

Energy in equals energy out.

How to create hydrogen? Electrolysis is the process used for pulling hydrogen from water, but it's only 38% efficient. Using fossil fuels would require over 2½ times the energy we now spend – which makes no sense. Some companies (in Canada & UK) are working on small units that use solar power to create the hydrogen. Storing the hydrogen is doable, but not easy ... as it's the smallest element.

Generating power from hydrogen does work nicely.

So – the jury is still out on power storage ...

Purdue University just produced a device that converts waste – organic and inorganic – to electricity, with a byproduct of ash that can be used in the soil. Such a device could lead to a reduced need for batteries, as well as provide a means of solid waste disposal. Just turn it on when the sun's down and there's no wind.

Perhaps we'll use batteries, short-term, then solar-produced hydrogen when available. Or – perhaps a combination of batteries and waste-to-power generators will do the best job. Power storage needs to be studied to see which type – or combination of types – fits best with a totally sustainable community.

Storing water will depend on geography.

The first Garden Atriums use cisterns, which provide more than enough water. A sustainable community might combine the cistern volume and create a reservoir – which could also be used for growing fish and for recreational and aesthetic purposes. Ultraviolet radiation and reverse osmosis filters can be used as water enters each house, eliminating the need for buying bottled water.

Most water is used for hose bibs and toilets. Moving away from grass lawns to landscape materials not requiring chemicals and constant watering has a huge impact. Moving to waterless toilets will also help – if people are ready to make that transition. (If they're not, stay with water, as the other could hurt sales.)

A community in a hilly area might opt to create a small reservoir for storing both rainwater and potential energy, power.

Community-sized wastewater systems are readily available. The positive outcome: gray water for agricultural irrigation; sludge for compost ... for food and gardens. Some intriguing perceptions and water management systems come from *"Growing Clean Water"* by Dr. B. C. Wolverton and John D. Wolverton ...

- The 21st century will feature buildings having their own microenvironments, with natural ecosystems to treat waste and purify the air.

- Less than 0.1 percent of all available fresh water remains for lakes, creeks, streams, rivers, and rainfalls. It's enough to meet our needs – but – it must be used again and again.

- Until the 20th century, the world's population took some 600,000 years to reach 1.6 billion. Since then, it has increased to over 6 billion. By 2050, 4 billion people will likely lack sufficient water.

- Toxins are also more prevalent in water than ever before. Because of multiple exposures to synthetic chemicals on a daily basis, it is nearly impossible to identify specific substances associated with cancer. Unheard of until the last century ...

Cancer is now the leading cause of disease-related death among children in the U.S. Childhood cancers are rising at the alarming rate of approximately 10 percent each year! In 1876, less than one-third of 1 percent of Americans died of cancer. Now, over 500,000 annually die of cancer.

- Making use of treated or partially treated water must become common practice. Nature has proven its innate ability to cleanse itself. The harnessing of these powers is a use whose time has come.

Studies have shown that aquatic plants – such as bulrush, duckweed, water hyacinths, cattail, and reed – excrete a variety of substances that act as bactericides, fungicides, and algaecides. While substances excreted from plant roots kill pathogenic bacteria, they are not harmful to microflora commonly found in the rhizosphere. In this way, domestic wastewater can serve as a complete hydroponic fertilizer for growing such vegetables as cherry tomatoes or green beans, and ...

Tertiary level wastewater treatment has resulted after only seven days. Phytotechnologies can be a viable wastewater treatment option, while also producing valuable byproducts such as crops; animal feed; and raw materials for industrial manufacturing applications. Nature has provided the means for us to treat our waste with a safe, economical alternative to engineered mechanical systems.

Technically, septic tanks of appropriate size enable solids to settle to the bottom. The fluid flowing from those tanks then passes through "rock/plant" filters ... long channels sized for the volume needed. 12 inches or less of wastewater is covered by 406 inches of rocks. The plants grow without soil. A wastewater contact time of 48 hours can achieve tertiary level treatment.

Thanks to the U.S. space program, which fostered Dr. Wolverton's NASA research, this system of natural wastewater treatment is emerging as the method of choice for small towns and communities all over the world. The system seems to cost about one-fourth the cost of a mechanical system, operates at a fraction of the cost of a mechanical system, and provides valuable crop assets.

Dr. Wolverton has already tested the system in multiple applications, including an entire town in southwest Virginia. This may be the most promising approach to treating wastewater in a sustainable village.

Solid waste management and recycling systems already exist. They need less innovation – other than adaptation for small communities. County planners indicate that whatever passes the state's health department is just fine with them.

In terms of "basics" such as toilet options that are more sustainable, Barker & Erickson cite two technologies that are relevant for waste treatment ...

1. Clivus Multrum. This is a waterless toilet that converts household (kitchen and bathroom) waste into compost and fertilizer right at the house. It kills pathogenic bacteria, so it can be used for enriching gardens. (Mainstream residents may not be ready for waterless toilets, however, no matter how good.)

2. TDP. The Thermal Depolymerization Process makes "waste" products into energy assets. Invented by Changing World Technologies, in Philadelphia, it can convert any carbon-based waste into burnable gas, fuel oil, and minerals suitable for manufacturing. Works with old tires, knocked-down houses, old computers, and organic waste. Devices for using trash to produce fuel may eliminate the need for batteries or fuel cells, for creating nighttime power.

Composting reduces waste disposal and contributes to the agricultural operation.

The problem?

We're all a little lazy.

Placing waste that can be composted into a container (e.g., a pail) must be easy, such as a bin at the kitchen sink, next to the trash can. People won't carry the pail a block or two. It may have to be gathered by a "compost collector" ... someone who goes house-to-house, accesses the compost bin from outside the house, and swaps a clean bin for a full one. The easier it is, the more people will participate.

Recycling needs to be made about that easy, as well.

And that brings us to the end of my initial research into the dimensions that Trina and I had identified as being critical to sustainable living. It's time for a ...

Summary

Pulling all these dimensions together, here's the start of an emerging picture ...

When the first Garden Atrium site is complete, we should have seed money to begin the next venture. We'll need a farm of 75-90 or so acres. That's enough land for 150 people, in 68 homes, and 50 acres for providing for 100% of everyone's food needs. Following the "Rule of 150," it's large enough to provide for population diversity, and small enough to be manageable, for a prototype effort.

Homes will be clustered. The village is surrounded by farmland. Homes will likely have PV power. Atop a hill, the community might have a wind machine and small reservoir. A pond at the bottom stores water, and is used for aquaculture. (The aquaculture people prefer three ponds, so that any sick fish can be isolated.) Water features are also used for recreation – gazebos, canoes, etc.

Coming from off-site, residents and their guests need to be able to drive to their homes – with garages and on-street parking – as that's what they expect. Movement within the village would be walking, biking, and – where needed – electric carts. Movement in the agricultural area would be by foot, electric cart, (or horse.)

On a longer-term basis, because cars are actually in use for very few hours a day, the community might eventually have a small fleet of vehicles, which can be leased hourly to residents. Most would be electric. And people could enjoy variety, depending on need and mood. A truck might be needed for hauling; a convertible for a nice day. Leased vehicles can be depreciated via a non-profit homeowners' association, further reducing costs to residents. To stay "normal" ...

Ideas such as this would likely come into use later.

Recreational uses can be made of lanes between crops as well as the hillside. That accommodates walking, jogging, horseback riding, and biking. Some site areas can also be designated for recreation, such as tennis or basketball courts.

The inn must be an easy walk from any home, ¼ mile maximum ... but preferably 250 feet or so. The village center needs "uses of interest" – which need to be defined by the residents. The decision process needs full participation in a consensus-building system. However ...

The village is not large enough to support a commercial enterprise, such as Starbucks. The best way to create a gathering place *and* a way for residents to have additional guest rooms available, when needed, may be a country inn. The inn would likely have 6-8 sleeping rooms, two meeting rooms. One would accommodate 30 to 50 or so, for use by residents for short courses, weddings and birthday celebrations, Christmas parties, film festivals, string quartets, or any other activity requiring space for that number. It would also have a smaller meeting room ...

This room would be for business meetings, for small groups – such as a book club – or for small group educational sessions.

The inn also must have dining facilities, such as a coffee shop, for guests and community residents. When people plan to get together for some reason – or just bump into one another – the easiest place to meet is a small coffee shop.

Having guest rooms at the inn is key to enabling people to enjoy and pay less, for smaller homes. Why pay for the space, then heat it or cool it, decorate it and maintain it, when it's used only one to three nights a month? Guests, when they're tired, could readily walk a couple of hundred feet, and stay at the inn, which caters to guests. You could still pay the costs – which would be a fraction of what it would cost to have extra guest rooms at your home.

Once we have an inn with guest rooms, we also need a kitchen – as its "B&B." And that enables us to have a small coffee shop for breakfasts.

If we find a chef, the food facility can also be a gathering place for mornings or evenings, a place for Sunday brunch, or even a place for dining out when residents don't feel like cooking. The inn might also advertise to outsiders, as a true country experience can be a delightful weekend getaway for people living in nearby cities.

> In Virginia, country inns typically enjoy a much higher occupancy than hotels or motels. Yet, while they are in the countryside, they aren't usually on a farm, with crops and chickens and cows and horses. Many people with whom we shared this vision have commented that outsiders would likely flock to such an inn, to experience what a farm is like ... and that if they were at all looking for another home, the experience itself might be the best sales tool.

The inn needs to also provide a space for sundries (in case someone runs out of toothpaste,) mail, UPS and Fed Ex, and convenience services, such as dry cleaning or shopping. In fact, the lobby, as a "crossroads" space with a concierge, seems to be increasingly key to making the village a truly exciting place in which to live.

Physical designs need to have an elegance that suggests:

"Sustainability" is a lot more than "survival."

Designs can be expressed through architecture, through delightful walkways, and through commanding gardens and ancillary features. In John W. Reps' *"The Making of America"* comes a description of open spaces ...

> *"In the layout of gardens we find the same techniques Renaissance architects advocated for the design of new towns and the reconstruction of old. The use of major and minor axes, the introduction of buildings, fountains or statues as terminal points of major circulation routes, and ...*

*... **the planning of open spaces at intervals, to add interest and variety.** These features were shared by town and garden design."*

According to J. B. Jackson, a foremost scholar of the American landscape ...

> "In the last generation we've lost the assurance and capacity, or the temerity, to contrive Utopias. It's no use trying to resurrect vanishing forms, beautiful though they may have been; their philosophical justification is gone. All we can do now is produce landscapes for unpredictable men where free and democratic intercourse of the Jeffersonian landscape can combine with the intense self-awareness of the solitary Romantic."

Bottom line, as people experience the community, they need to conclude ...

"This feels like a great place in which to live!"

In a sense, the community needs to be an *inspiring* environment. It needs to convert the fear that Peak Oil spin-offs will trigger into positive energy. The site needs a vista ... a view that gives it a sense of "place" ... the place to be.

This second generation of Garden Atriums may be even more of a departure from "the usual" than the first. Regardless of how well everything works, or how glorious everything looks, we're back at Square #1, trying to attract cultural creative early adapters. The test needs to occur in a geography that is experiencing growth – which leaves the northern states out, except for a city that has in-migration.

For example, the corridor along U.S. 29 from Charlottesville to Washington, D.C., has in-migration that should continue for years, and a fairly progressive attitude. Charlottesville has an airport, a train station, several medical centers and universities, and is two hours from Washington, D.C. Eastern West Virginia and the eastern Pennsylvania hills – not far from Hagerstown, Maryland – offer similar in-migration and amenities. The biggest questions, then ...

How to test the vision's marketability?

What features would make it *more* marketable?

One idea, from Jeremy Heyes of WATG, the world's leading planner and designer of resort and leisure developments ...

> *"The project needs an established and respected brand. For example, if it carries the name Ritz-Carlton, people will instantly see all the innovations as positive and well done. Plus – a resort operator knows how to run reservations, food service, concierge services, housekeeping and maintenance, etc. And ...*

"They could rent unsold spec houses, by the day, week or month ... until they are sold."

Because the effort is new and therefore untested, any simulations or methods for increasing the odds of success and reducing risk are welcome ... and essential!

One pragmatic question for making a sustainable community real, and a critical question for selling this model of sustainable living, is ...

> Who will make a (very high-end) buying decision *now*,
> based on likely (but not guaranteed) future events?

I believe, from all the data I've been tracking for many years, that huge changes are going to be happening ... and soon. I also do not have a crystal ball. If we can live as we've been living, and if government solves all the financial and environmental problems we're experiencing – such that sustainability is no longer an issue – then we'd all be more comfortable enjoying life as we have been.

Preventive medicine is a "tough sell." All the research says that if we get an annual physical, we'll enjoy better health and live a longer, more comfortable life. But ...

> How many of us do have annual physicals ... each and every year?

> And how many of us will make these major life changes
> to become more sustainable before it's too late?

James Smith, a health economist at the RAND Corporation, surveyed research related to longevity. The only factor he found to consistently parallel longevity – regardless of income level, race, ethnicity, or nationality – was the *level of education*.

> *"You have to be willing to do something that is not pleasant now,*
> *and you have to stay with it and think about the future."*

People with higher levels of education somehow seem better able to delay gratification. In sustainability, by the time the supermarket no longer has any fish, or by the time oxygen levels drop too low to support healthy living, conditions may be irreversible. While it seems unfair to target demographic groups with greater levels of education, the people most likely to be buyers of a new concept in sustainable living may be those with more education.

Seeking geographies in which the education levels are higher – or university campuses that have sufficient land for agricultural research – may make more sense.

In Ervin Laszlo's *"The Chaos Point,"* he sees current civilization, the industrial civilization, coming to a close and evolving either into a new level of civilization, or ... into a breakdown of society.

For instance ...

The Window of Decision, 2005 – 2012, is the third phase in what appears to be a regular evolution that mankind has gone through, from era to era. In his words ...

> "The dominant social order is stressed by radically changing conditions that place in question established values, worldviews, ethics and aspirations. Society enters a period of ferment. Now the flexibility and creativity of the people create that subtle but all-important 'fluctuation' that decides which of the available paths of development society will hereafter take."

The Chaos Point, 2012, is the fourth and final phase ...

> "The processes initiated at the dawn of the nineteenth century and accelerating since the 1960s build inevitably toward a decision-window and then toward a critical threshold of no return, the Chaos Point. Now a simple rule holds: We cannot stand still; we cannot go back; we must keep moving. There are alternative ways we can keep moving forward. There is a path to breakdown, as well as a path to a new world."

Adding to that pattern ...

> *"The central bankers know that the alternative to a gradual if painful adjustment is the radical step of switching to another reserve currency. If they do, the U.S. would no longer be able to finance its deficit in dollars, and the American economy would face a shock similar to that which led to the collapse of the Argentine economy. This would have worldwide repercussions."* (Complementary currency seems needed.)

And ...

> *"The IMF's 2005 'Economic Outlook' noted that it is no longer a question of whether the world economy will adjust, only how it will adjust. If measures required for a gradual adjustment are delayed, the adjustment will be 'abrupt.' It will be a part, or perhaps a trigger, of the Chaos Point faced by the entire world economy."*

Then Laszlo looks at what's needed in the way of a transformation ...

> *"Einstein was right; the problems created by the prevalent way of thinking cannot be solved by the same way of thinking. This is a crucial insight. Without renewing our culture and consciousness we will be unable to transform today's dominant civilization and overcome the problems generated by its shortsighted mechanistic and manipulative thinking.*

And ...

"We know that a viable new civilization must evolve a culture and consciousness very different from the mindset that characterized most of the twentieth century.

"Extensive growth moves along a horizontal plane on the surface of the planet: It conquers ever more territories, colonizes ever more people, and imposes the will of the dominant layers on ever more layers of the population.

"Intensive growth, on the other hand, centers on the development of individuals, and of the communities and ecologies in which they live.

"Extensive growth generates unsustainability: it drives the world toward chaos.

"Intensive growth could produce sustainability: it could drive contemporary societies toward a new mode of functioning – a new civilization.

"The paramount end of extensive growth can be encapsulated in three "C's" ...

      'conquest, colonization, and consumption.'

"In intensive growth, the end is very different. It can be grasped under three other "C's ...

      'connection, communication, and consciousness.'

"Evolution focused on the growth of connection, communication, and consciousness could create a fundamental shift in the civilization that dominates life on this planet. It could drive the next transformation in a positive direction, from Logos to Holos."

The factors that have evolved in considering a community that can live sustainably – but live well – seem consistent with Laszlo's views. All the more reason that such a development needs to be attempted. And the time to act – or not act – is *now!*

"We can also make clear that abiding by a universal morality does not entail undue sacrifice. Living in a way that enables all others to live as well does not mean being self-denying. We can continue to strive for excellence and beauty, personal growth and enjoyment, even for comfort and luxury. But when we are guided by universal moral principles, we define the pleasures and achievements of life in relation to the quality of enjoyment and level of satisfaction they provide, rather than in terms of the amount of money they cost and the quantity of materials and energy their production and use call for. In 1968, when Robert Kennedy was running for the presidential nomination he said ...

'Some men see things as they are and say, why?
I dream things that never were and say, why not?'

*"To dream the world as you wish to see it is never just to indulge an idle
fancy. Today, living in a window in time that decides our future, it has
more relevance than ever. Margaret Mead said,*

> *'Never doubt the power of a small group of people to
> change the world. Nothing else ever has.'*

"Mahatma Gandhi was even more insistent:

> *'Be the change you want to see in the world.'*

*"They were right. When you evolve your consciousness, you have the
power to change the world.*

*"Why is consciousness so potent? The explanation is at hand: In a
decision-window, even small 'fluctuations' can change the destiny of
the system. A fluctuation in the form of a more evolved consciousness is
particularly powerful. A more evolved consciousness means new thinking, and is the key to a new civilization. A new civilization, in turn, is
the key to well-being, and even the survival of humankind."*

While my initial motivation behind this second sustainable housing venture was
physiological sustainability – heating, cooling, power, food, etc. – the research involved in developing the idea has carried my initial thinking way beyond its original
intentions. Somehow, quality-of-life feelings, happiness, and aesthetics all began to
be woven into the picture.

And somehow, all this thinking fits astonishing well with the kind of thinking em-
bodied in Laszlo's work. (And – Dr. Laszlo is a physicist who does a lot of work with
wave theory. He deals with the physical universe, and isn't a "metaphysical" type.)
Nonetheless, the need seems unquestionably there, and strikingly immediate ...

> *"At a decision-window, individuals can consciously create the small
> but potentially powerful fluctuations that could 'blow up' and decide
> the evolutionary path their society will adopt. They can tip the system
> toward the evolution that is in line with their hopes and expectations.
> Thus, the Chaos Point need not be the harbinger of global breakdown.
> It could be the herald of a leap to a new civilization."*

If "evolved consciousness" is essential in this coming evolution, how, specifically, do
we turn that ideal into a reality? And what is "evolved consciousness" anyway?

Addressing a joint session of the U.S. Congress in February of 1991, Vaclav Havel,
then the president of Czechoslovakia, said ...

"Without a global revolution in the sphere of human consciousness, nothing will change for the better ... and the catastrophe towards which this world is headed – the ecological, social, demographic, or general breakdown of civilization – will be unavoidable."

This scenario can be avoided. Human consciousness is already evolving. Adapted from *The Chaos Point* are ten benchmarks of an "evolved consciousness" ...

1. Live in ways that enable all other people to live as well, satisfying your needs without detracting from the chances of other people to satisfy theirs.

2. Live in ways that respect the lives of others and that respect the right to the economic and cultural development of all people, wherever they live and whatever their ethnic origin, sex, citizenship, station in life, and belief system.

3. Live in ways that safeguard the intrinsic right to living and to an environment supportive of life for all the things that live and grow on Earth.

4. Pursue happiness, freedom, and personal fulfillment in harmony with the integrity of nature and with consideration for the similar pursuits of others in society.

5. Require that your government relate to other nations and peoples peacefully and in a spirit of cooperation, recognizing the legitimate aspirations for a better life and a healthy environment of all the people in the human family.

6. Require business enterprises to accept responsibility for all their stakeholders as well as for the sustainability of their environment, demanding that they produce goods and offer services that satisfy legitimate demand without impairing nature and reducing the opportunities of smaller and less privileged entrants to compete in the same marketplace.

7. Require public media to provide a constant stream of reliable information on basic trends and crucial processes to enable you and other citizens and consumers to reach informed decisions on issues that affect your and their life and well-being.

8. Make room in your life to help those less privileged than you to live a life of dignity, free from the struggles and humiliations of abject poverty.

9. Encourage young people and open-minded people of all ages to evolve the spirit that could empower them to ...

... make ethical decisions of their own on issues that decide their future and the future of their children.

10. Work with like-minded people to preserve or restore the essential balances of the environment, with attention to your neighborhood, your country or region, and the whole of the biosphere.

Some of these ten benchmarks are likely qualities that will emerge from the kind of sustainable community being envisioned. Some – such as controlling a larger government, businesses, or the media – are clearly beyond the purview of a small community ... though residents can certainly be advocates and attempt to influence. Even so, an "evolved consciousness" may be a difficult trait to measure ...

"Are we evolved yet?"

Dr. Anne Adams' research provides additional guidelines for helping people develop an evolved consciousness. She begins with a definition by Allan Combs ...

"The ability to enter into cooperative exchanges with others while retaining a complete and developed awareness of one's own individuality."

Both individual and collective goals need to be acknowledged and honored. More specifically, here are four domains of consciousness. Each needs to evolve:

1. Consciousness in the physical domain.

This aspect of consciousness is discernible in the relationship a person has with his or her own body. There is a relationship – a depth of knowing, feeling, and appreciation; a partnership. There is "communication" occurring throughout the body; one "listens" to the body's cues and requirements and respects its messages. Physical awareness is a dynamic, direct, and interactive relationship with life – not only a conceptual "knowing about."

2. Consciousness in the emotional domain.

Consciousness as awareness, attentiveness, knowledge, understanding, and "presence" shows up in the emotional domain as deep connection – an individual with himself or herself; with his or her family, community, peers, friends, teachers, etc. Being known, loved, listened to, respected, and self-expressed, allows a human being to be present and engaged in his or her life. Being "emotionally conscious" also manifests in the ability to demonstrate plasticity, "dance" with many different kinds of people, and anticipate situations and their possible consequences.

3. Consciousness in the mental domain, which is ...

Consciousness as awareness, attentiveness, knowledge, understanding, and "presence" makes itself known in the mental domain as a natural expression of being human. When human beings are given the opportunity to discover their own relationship with learning, through their own unique ...

passion
choices
curiosity
expression
experiences
and embodiment ...

... their consciousness expands as a result of their "presence" throughout the learning process. Consciousness is seen in mental intelligence as a high level of flexibility and ease of engagement exhibited in the way ideas are interconnected. Awareness expresses itself through contextual thinking; how individuals discriminate, interpret, draw conclusions, and communicate; their ability to see larger patterns and grasp the "whole picture" and honor the interconnectedness of all life.

4. Consciousness in the spiritual domain.

Consciousness as awareness, attentiveness, knowledge, understanding, and "presence" appears in the spiritual domain in the quality of meaning, purpose, and values an individual creates for his or her life. A spiritually aware person embodies the interconnectedness of all life and sees himself or herself in relation to a larger world, connected with themselves, others, and nature.

Educating for an evolved consciousness would provide experiences in *each* sphere of intelligence that are interwoven from the beginning of life.

Most of Laszlo's ten qualities for an evolved consciousness can be readily supported with the concepts built into this new sustainable community. Achieving an "evolved consciousness" in these other four ways may still be a matter of question.

Much has been written about the potential devastation that's anticipated to happen in the near future ...

- climate change;

- widespread starvation;

- dying off of many species;

- increased seismic activity;

- terrorists taking over the world; and ...

- increasing storm frequency and severity;

- financial collapse of the United States; and ...

- financial collapse of the world.

The predictions come from sources as varied as ancient Mayan writings to some of the top scientists of our times. They fill our media. Some may happen. All may happen. The theme in most of these writings is: **Fear!** ... with few or no solutions.

From *Chaos Point, Apocalypse 2012,* and other readings, major change forecasts seem both consistent and imminent. Whether from volcanic activity, tsunamis, earthquakes, or comets ... major problems are seen in the offing. The good news:

> **Virtually every source sees the trauma signaling the end of one era of humanity, followed by the beginning of a new – and very *positive* – age of evolution of our species.**

These likely major upheavals and changes do beg the question ...

> Does "sustainable development" have any meaning, really?

Seen in the broader perspective that's evolved in the course of my research – well beyond heating, cooling, electricity, water, air quality, and other physiological factors – I sense the answer is ...

> ***"Yes."***

New communities may help people evolve in ways that are appropriate to what seems to be a whole new era for our human evolution.

My question, from a development perspective, is ...

> "In the context of all these very likely upheavals,
> how can this development work, financially?"

- Creating smaller, more affordable homes may have special sales and financing advantages.

- The entire community, including the utility systems, may need to be created in "pay as you go" phases, which diminishes indebtedness.

- Smaller units may be able to be purchased with no mortgage whatever.

- Pre-sales provides development capital, reduces or eliminates indebtedness, and ensures more sales for the first phase. Then ...

- Once the farm, inn, and initial homes exist, the rest can grow incrementally, to control risk exposure.

Following the guidelines surfaced in the course of this research, living in this community should help residents achieve the transition that seems essential to our ability to sustain. The community can also serve as a model ... an idea from which to learn, that can be copied and modified by others, so that sustainable living can evolve and grow.

One final thought from the research I did ...

Like it or not, we're living in a time of major change. Old systems – and leaders of those systems – no matter how dysfunctional they've become, don't die without a fight. And – the old system is all we know; it's what we've depended on our entire life. Change brings with it high levels of uncertainty. And uncertainty and anxiety can give rise to ...

Fear!

Roosevelt was right ...

The only thing we have to fear is fear itself. We need to see the changes that seem to inevitably be coming as ...

A Magnificent <u>Opportunity</u>!

We need to follow all the logic that says, sustainable living is truly what we need. And we need to see this evolution as much more than ways to provide food, clothing, and shelter. We really need to have the courage to "go with the flow" that seems to be unquestionably happening, and to realize a ...

<u>Better</u> quality of living
than we could have ever imagined!

Neil Armstrong's famous words, upon stepping down onto the moon's surface for the first time ... *"That's one small step for man; one giant leap for mankind."* ... symbolized a great moment for our entire planet. Learning to live sustainably, in the full sense that's evolved with this research, seems to also be a truly new frontier, and might be seen as an even *more* momentous leap for our entire human civilization. And that's "Sustainability" ...

> Living in harmony with the earth and all that reside here – trees, animals, insects, humans, and soil – with none dominating another. It's a partnership that honors and values all.

That's "sustainability" as I knew it at the end of the research I conducted. But ...

Research, from a standpoint of learning, never really ends. In the past year or so, a series of events that occurred throughout my life culminated in a whole new perspective about what's happening. It doesn't belie the research, because when I see data from multiple independent sources pointing in the same direction, it's usually very reliable. Rather, it's given a whole new meaning to what's really happening.

What I was exploring and reporting, you might see as "symptoms."

What I (somehow) slid into in the past eighteen months or so gets into the root causes ... why we're about to undergo the huge transformations we'll be experiencing. If you think what I've shared so far went further than you thought sustainability went, this next part, for me, really went off the "deep end" ...

Circa 2008: Going Where Mankind Has Not Gone Before

I don't know about your life experiences, but I have to say that my life has been a "wayward adventure" ... though I've since learned that there are *no* accidents.

As I mentioned earlier, I have two undergraduate degrees, one in architecture and one in structural engineering. Both of those disciplines are focused on physical aspects ... creating our "built environment." My sensitivities were much greater in dealing with form, color, and texture than they were with "human stuff," such as feelings ... or interpersonal communication.

What does emotion have to do with great architecture?

What does emotion have to do with selecting
the right structure for a roof?

In retrospect, I guess I was awkward in many social situations. Maybe not as bad as was depicted in *"Revenge of the Nerds,* but probably in that general direction.

My master's degree was in architecture, with a focus on urban design ... and what does all that "sappy" emotion have to do with the texture of a neighborhood or the landscape of a waterfront or parkway? In fact, I began working in early computer graphics, to try to simulate movement through an urban area ... to enable designers to make adjustments, and experience those adjustments, to beautify cities.

My career was seeming to be research focused, including writing my own software. And what does emotion have to do with any of that? Then I thought ...

> *"If I'm destined to be a researcher, which seems fun and satisfying, I should probably get a Ph. D. ... a research degree.*

I was then a young assistant professor at the University of Nebraska. On campus was an exposition of educational architecture, so I floated over there, out of curiosity. There, I began chatting with a Dr. Donald Leu, a professor at Michigan State University. Dr. Leu said he needed someone with my background on his school facility planning team, and that – while I had to take tests and fill out forms – I was accepted. And – he said he'd make sure that "education" didn't get in the way of "real education."

That was intriguing. So I filled out the forms that came to me, took the required tests, and ... was accepted. For the next year and a half, I continued university teaching and research, and took courses that I could transfer to MSU. When I got on campus, in a department of organization development (housed in a college of education,) one of the "rages" that was going around was ...

Sensitivity Training!

Dr. John Suehr, one of the members of my doctoral committee, was reputed to be some kind of a guru in sensitivity training, so I asked him what it was all about.

"It would be good for you."

That's all could get from him ... along with a kind of "all-knowing guru smile." Between the next quarters was a ten-day sensitivity training "laboratory" – so off I went. A "T-Group," as they were called, had ten participants and two trainers. In total, there were a dozen such groups, in adjoining rooms ... which enabled some large-group exercises in the evenings. There I was, looking at eleven strangers, when one of the trainers asked ...

"How are you feeling?"

And my answer, quite naturally, was ...

"I'm feeling fine."

"Talk more about your feelings."

"I'm feeling really fine."

And for ten days, the twelve of us sat around the room talking about our feelings. I have to admit that it was a bit of a traumatic experience for me. (For those of you reading this who are technically-oriented, I think you'll relate to my discomfort. For those of you reading this who have a more humanistic background and skill set, you're probably having a good laugh.) But I have to admit, I began to see a few things more clearly. And I guess I had to admit that maybe feelings were more relevant than I'd thought ... at least in some arenas.

I'd been in meetings in which I could sense "something isn't clicking" or "there seems to be some kind of game going on." But I was pretty oblivious to all that stuff ... until the T-Group experience. (I'm actually still not great ... but better.)

That began opening a new world for me.

It was a world that was *not* physical. No form, color or texture. It was emotional.

But ... it *was* real.

I never became as skilled in seeing and addressing feelings as others I've met and with whom I've worked, but at least I recognized the dimension and had some skill.

If you think that's a big shift, wait until you see this next one.

Skipping forward about twenty years ...

My eldest son was graduating from college. As he and some of the young men and women with whom he shared an off-campus house were changing into their caps and gowns, parents were waiting on the front porch. I began chatting with one of the other fathers, and somehow – and I have no idea how – the subject of "spirit" and the "non-physical universe of which we're a part" came up.

It wasn't a religious discussion in any way, but I'd always sensed that our lives must be a part of some larger system ... "the universe," or whatever. I was curious.

This other father said he'd read an article about some guy in Virginia who was exploring the non-physical domains, and he said he'd send me the article ... which he did. And that began a whole new "domain of exploration" ...

The explorer was Robert Monroe.

I heard that Monroe had been a radio mogul in New York, but really liked experimenting with things. He knew, from research, that the left and right hemispheres of our brain are a few megahertz apart. He wondered what might happen if he split the sound frequencies, and had people listen with stereo headsets ... so that the two hemispheres of the brain would come to the same frequency. Paraphrasing from my memory of one of his presentations ...

> "After tinkering with the system for most of the day, I eventually turned in. Then, during the night, I awoke and found myself on the floor, next to a fountain. So I looked around the room, and on the ceiling was my bed. And my wife was in it. And so was I.
>
> "I was on the ceiling. The fountain was really our chandelier. And I was out of my body, and all I could think about was getting back into my body. And – zap – I was back.
>
> "Then I got curious about where I might be able to go and what I might be able to learn. And as long as I knew I could get back into my body whenever I so wished, I was OK on exploring and seeing what I could discover. So I kept a notepad next to my bed, and began my explorations into ... who knew where."

Monroe then sold all his radio assets and bought a site about thirty minutes southwest of Charlottesville, Virginia. He built a home for himself, and three buildings for his new "Monroe Institute."

- One building is a laboratory, in which he could continue all sorts of exploration experiments. Monroe was a hearty man and an entrepreneur, not a "psychic," and – most of all – he was an explorer.

- Another building was designed for special classes ...

- It has sleeping spaces for 24 people. Usually, two people share a room. Within it, each has what's call a "Check Unit," a roomette the size of a twin bed mattress, can be totally darkened, has an ideal temperature, and is equipped with stereo headsets and a tape recorder, so people can record their experiences. The building also has a large room, for total class briefings, and a dining facility.

- The third building has a large hall for total group presentations, and break-out rooms, for special exercises; it's used in the evenings.

As I mentioned earlier, I've always been one of those *"Ya pays yer nickel and ya takes yer chances"* types, so I signed up for my first course. It's called "Gateway." It begins on a Saturday afternoon and ends after breakfast the following Friday. So off I went to the Monroe Institute ... which eventually made the sensitivity training experience seem like ho-hum pablum.

Each "session" uses one of the institute's "Hemi-Synch" audio tapes. You get a briefing in the large space, beforehand. Then ... off to your Check Unit. When you're lying down, comfortable, and have your headset on, you press your "Ready" button. When everyone's done so, they begin a tape – which I'd guess is about 45 minutes long. (They confiscate all watches at the outset, so we live with the sun.)

I still remember my first tape. They have you relax, do some humming, to create a relaxed vibration, then – basically – nothing. The rest of the tape sounds like white noise. So ... I had a relaxing experience, with a vision of ... *black*! Eyes closed in my darkened Check Unit, and I saw ... nothing. Towards the end of the tape, they talk you "down" (from wherever some people may have been.) And back to the large room, where people could share their experiences.

I naturally didn't share anything, as "blackness" would not add much to the dialogue. But some others reported out-of-body experiences. Some had (what I like to call) "intergalactic experiences." Some had fascinating visions and messages. I finally asked the trainers ...

"Were we all listening to the <u>same</u> tape?"

They indicated that different people have different experiences from the same tape. And the people reporting these unusual experiences weren't "weird" types ... just seemingly normal people from all over and from different background. They really weren't trying to put on a show to impress others in the class.

I noticed some others said nothing. I asked them afterwards about their experience, and it was similar to mine ... blackness! I thought I was in for a week of rest.

Later in the week, we had a tape that was supposed to give us the easiest way to go out-of-body ... which really was not one of my goals. That was an experience ...

The tape relaxed us, as usual. First, we went to what they call "Level 10," which is defined as "body asleep, mind totally awake." It's just a basic state of relaxation. Then the trainer helps us to what the institute calls "Level 12" – an expanded consciousness. Not sure what that is, exactly, except I do get a tingling line across my right cheek when I'm at that level, so I must have been doing something right. Then Monroe's soothing radio voice comes on and said something like ...

> "Imagine you're lying down on the bottom of a canoe. You're out in the middle of a very still lake ... no wind or waves at all.
>
> "Now I want you to rock gently to your left, then to your right, and then – after a few more repetitions ... just roll over and stand up.

Well ... I went through the exercise, but never could stand up. So I decided to just relax and enjoy a few more minutes of comfortable, quiet blackness. Later, his voice returned and began talking us down to Level One ... the normal awake state.

As we "came down" ... I could sense my right foot tapping against my left knee. This was not subtle. My legs, like everyone's, are essentially the same length and I was lying down on my back. How could my foot touch my knee?

As soon as we got down to Level One, I turned on the light in my Check Unit to see what had happened. My legs were the same length. Then, a "thought" hit me ...

> "Right now, an out-of-body experience would be too frightening for you, but we wanted you to know the phenomenon is real. So ... we gave you an out-of-leg experience!"

Some people in the class would see pictures – like in a dream. Some would get messages typed across their dark vision. Some would hear a voice talking to them. I got "a sense" ... "a thought." Here I am, in a domain that's way out of my "form, color, texture" element, and getting just very subtle "senses" instead of something more concrete. I couldn't tell if I were just imagining it or if it was real. In fact ...

Later in the week I did ask, at the start of one tape, for some kind of concrete verification. My body immediately swelled up and I let loose with one of the biggest farts I can remember! And what I "sensed" was laughter. Well, I wasn't having any intergalactic voyages or even more modest out-of-body experiences. But by the end of the week I did have a sense that ...

1. "Something" is, indeed, there; and ...

2. It has a wild sense of humor!

I've never thought of "spirit" as having a wild sense of humor? Is that "divine"?

But, "something" was there. It wasn't a zero. So, a year later ...

I went back for a second course, "Guidelines." Now that term, to an architect, means a pair of parallel lines between which you letter notes on drawings. Monroe had his own definition. Paraphrasing from memory ...

> *"Each of us has an 'inner being' that's really the non-physical part of who we are. Some call it their 'higher self.' We'll just call it your 'Inner Self Helper'...or 'ISH'."*

Monroe loved acronyms ... and the more humorous the better.

So we began a new set of briefings and tapes, and I was experiencing ... blackness! At the end of one of our briefings, I asked one of the trainers why I wasn't getting anything visual. The trainer simply said ...

> *"Tell ISH you want visuals."*

So, as the next tape began, I asked ISH for visuals. And during the tape I suddenly fell into what seemed like a dream – with visuals – and I suddenly thought ...

> *"Oh, no, I've gone to sleep."*

So I pushed away the dream and was clearly awake again. Then I got this sensing of roaring laughter and the thought ...

> *"You asked for visuals, I gave you visuals, and you pushed them away! Now what is it you really want?"*

Not all 24 students returned to the large space after each tape. One or two were usually missing, and joined the group after ten or twenty minutes. The trainers said that sometimes people "click out" – but – I wasn't going to pay my nickel, attend a class, and then sleep through it. No way! So ... I had to learn to simply trust ISH, and *relax*, and let ISH give me visual experiences.

My visuals are actually somewhat different than my dreams. I pop into them suddenly, as I do when I go to sleep. And I exit them either when I go to another visual or when the voice comes on to talk us down. But – where dreams fade, I can remember visuals I've had – at least the key ones – for years, and clearly.

Now I want to share a couple of experiences I had at "Guidelines" that have direct bearing on what's coming and on sustainability ...

My roommate's name was George. He was a janitor from Banff, Alberta, Canada. He had taken "Gateway" about ten years previously, but said that he had a vision that he was supposed to return to the Monroe Institute for a class called "Guidelines" that was being offered on a specific date. So, he phoned the institute, and it confirmed that, yes, there was a class by that name and on those dates. But he had limited funds. When he shared his vision with the institute, the person with whom he was speaking said ...

"If you can somehow get here, the course will be free to you."

On Saturday, after introductions, we did our first tape. And I had ... blackness. And George was ... "Mr. Intergalactic!" He was a very gentle, unpretentious man. But he had amazing experiences during those tapes! And he was always waiting for me to come out of my Check Unit and asked how my experience was.

Then, Monday morning, when I arose, I saw George at his little desk, drawing what looked like a very complex organic chemical configuration ... what I used to call, in my organic chemistry classes, "di-chloro-phenol-chickenwire." I asked George what he was drawing. (It was an elaborate grouping of phenol bonds.) He said ...

> *I don't know what it is; I've never had chemistry. But this is why I was supposed to be here. Someone will be coming here to ask me for this diagram.*

So – when George finished the diagram – comparing it to a vision he held in his head – we washed and headed for breakfast, which was on the lower floor of a two story space, with an overlooking balcony. Part way through our breakfast, some man who was not a student in the class appeared on the balcony and asked ...

> *"Is there someone here by the name of George?"*

George waved to him, and he came down the stairs and joined us. Then he said ...

> *"I'm a physician at the University of Virginia Medical Center. Last night, I had this strange dream that I was supposed to find a place called the Monroe Institute and ask for someone named George.*
>
> *"When I awoke, I searched and found that the Monroe Institute did exist and was only twenty minutes away. So I decided I'd pursue this strange experience and see if someone named George was here."*

George reached in his shirt pocket and gave the physician his diagram, saying ...

> *"I think this diagram is supposed to be for you."*

The physician almost "lost it."

> *"This week, I'm going to Boston to do some special cancer research. This diagram just answered some of the biggest problems I've been facing. This is amazing!"*

The physician left and we finished our breakfast. I knew I had witnessed something amazing, verifying for me that "something" is there. It isn't my imagination.

"Guidelines" got better for me, once I began to get visuals. Then, on the last day, on one of the last tapes we were to hear ...

I had two memorable visual experiences ...

> One explained a dream that's recurred all my life; it was an amazing
> explanation!

> The other visual was odd. I saw a log cabin in the woods, surrounded
> by fir trees. It was two stories and had no windows – except may-
> be a vertical slit window. There were no foundation plantings, and I
> couldn't tell if it was a home or a warehouse or what. I "sensed" it was
> sixty feet long and that the entrance was around the corner to my left
> (as I was viewing it.) And that was all. Is that odd?

At tape's end, I emerged from my Check Unit and there was George, asking if I'd had
some good experience.

> *"George, my first vision explained a dream I've had, again and again,*
> *all my life. It was amazing. The second was curious, though."* I de-
> scribed my image of the log cabin, and that I sensed it was sixty feet
> long and that the entrance was around the corner on the left side.

George responded with ...

> *"Yes, it is sixty feet long; I built it myself. And yes, the entrance is*
> *around the corner on the left side, from where you were viewing it."*

Now, how can that happen? I concluded that my ISH asked George's ISH for some
piece of data that I could only get that way, to let me know that all this is concrete.
After the class, George sent me a picture of his cabin from where I'd been viewing it
and it was a perfect match with my vision.

So, by the end of "Guidelines" I wasn't exactly "Mr. Intergalactic" – but – I did know,
for *sure*, that there is more to our world than meets the eye. And I became better able
to understand phenomena we often see as weird. For instance ...

> You've heard of instances in which a passenger, about to board a plane,
> hears a voice telling the person not to board that flight. (Then, later,
> that flight has problems.) Or ...

> A person going home, to his or her apartment in an apartment build-
> ing, hears a voice saying not to enter the building. (Soon afterward,
> violence is reported to have happened in the building.)

> The voice comes from their ISH. Normally, entities do not interfere
> with day-to-day human activity. But they may, in an emergency.

During the past ten years, Trina and I had been learning more and more about
"Sustainability." We had gone forward with our housing project, and ...

... on a general level, we were working towards living more sustainably, ourselves.

- We recycled as much as possible.

- We planted trees whenever we could.

- We ate as much locally grown food as we could.

- And we drove only one high-mileage car between us.

In general, we were trying to be sensitive to the footprint we were leaving on the earth, with our goal being to be as gentle as possible. What we began learning is ...

There's a connection between "spiritual" and "sustainable."

On http://planet2025.net/?page_id=1283, from Michael Ben-Eli, I saw the first published link of sustainability with the spiritual domain ...

> *"The human spirit has consistently sought to transcend material, biological, physiological, psychological, and technology limitations. This constant drive for touching a "beyond," for taking progressively more into the field of vision and integrating an increasingly broader "reality" has a huge practical significance. With its intuitive reach for wholeness and completion, it fuels the development and evolution of individuals and societies alike.*
>
> *"The extent to which this deeply rooted drive is actually allowed to manifest in the daily affairs of society, affects the choices we make and the quality of our actions in the world.*
>
> *"Ultimately, it underscores the difference between a greedy, ego-centric, predatory orientation and a nurturing, self-restrained, inclusive approach which honors the larger system of which we are a part and on which we depend for our very existence.*
>
> *"The essential quality of the spiritual domain, recognized, as it is, by all known wisdom traditions, is not easy to pin down. In the English language, the term spiritual carries opposing connotations: sacred, exalted, virtuous, divine, but also, insubstantial and occult. It is meant here to evoke a sense of a deep, underlying essence — a combination of inspiration, meaning, purpose, and a motivating, all encompassing value. The fundamental imprecision which is involved is manifest in the more elaborate way in which the fifth principle is expressed."*

The principles:

"Recognize the seamless, dynamic continuum of mystery, wisdom, love, energy, and matter that links the outer reaches of the cosmos with our solar system, our planet and its biosphere, including all humans, with our internal metabolic systems and their externalized technology extensions. Embody this recognition in a universal ethics for guiding human actions."

So ... while I began with physical aspects of sustainability – and we do need those items, so we're comfortable – my journey really expanded to quality of life and happiness and now even into "co-creative living."

Next, let's "fast forward" to very recent times and some experiences with a very astute, bright, and actually adventurous futurist, John Petersen ...

John is sort of a "data junkie" who also synthesizes the data and sees the trends ... where the data are heading. He's like a walking fountain of knowledge about where the world is going. His book, *"A Vision for 2012,"* is a great example. In a brief, easy-to-read book, he provides a terse but thorough picture of the major problems facing mankind. Then he balances the picture – which is very rare these days – with major technical innovations that may solve many of the problems.

Trina and I got to know John, through presentations his organization, the Arlington Institute, organized. In a kind of "by the bye," off-handed way, he will occasionally mention books he thought were both provocative and relevant to sustainability ... to where our world is really heading. The first I'll mention is ...

The Perelandra Garden Workbook, I and II, by Machaelle Small Wright. She was having experiences similar to those who founded the farm at Findhorn, Scotland.

If you're not familiar with Findhorn, Eileen and Peter Caddy, their three sons, and their friend, Dorothy MacLean, followed intuitive guidance to set up home and garden in windswept and barren sand dunes in the far northeast of Scotland. Their discovery of how to contact and co-operate with nature spirits and devas made the seemingly impossible possible. On a small plot of poor soil around a 30-foot trailer, the most wonderful flowers, vegetables, and fruit grew to *enormous* size.

Wright used her learnings in how to work with earth energies to create an amazing quantity and quality of product at her Perelandra gardens, in Virginia. Wright's gardening books are indeed a step-by-step approach. In making decisions, she uses kinesiology ... a process with which you may be familiar, as it's used by many physicians, chiropractors, homeopaths, and others who provide health-related services. The way it works is ...

You hold your thumb and pinky together, firmly.

Someone poses a yes/no question to you, as they try to separate your thumb from your pinky. And ...

If the answer is "Yes," you can easily resist their effort.

If the answer is "No," your thumb and pinky will separate easily.

Some medical practitioners ask you to hold out your arm, and will press down on it to sense resistance, to see if the answer is yes or no. Why does this work? Our body has an electrical system flowing through it ... an energy flow, if you will. A "Yes" allows that energy to continue flowing, where a "No" stops the flow and we lose muscle control, so our fingers separate or our arm easily drops.

The electric circuitry explanation seems reasonable, enough. Now comes what I'd call the big question ...

Who controls the electrical energy flow?

It actually depends on the question asked. When it comes to a garden, it's the energy of the earth, of the garden, of the soil, or even of a specific plant. It seems that we can communicate with plants or natural objects using kinesiology ... though a yes/no process can become tedious! And, if you've been doing it for a while, you don't know if your fingers separated from fatigue or because the answer was "No," so you need to work in short spurts.

But this process is known as "co-creative." Trina and I tried it in our vegetable garden, and the results that year – and every year since – have been amazing. While we can't ask ...

"What should we plant in our garden?"

... because it's not in a yes/no format, we can ask ...

"Should we plant carrots in Row #1?" "Row #2?" "Row #3?"
(It can be tedious.)

Whether or not you follow the "advice" that comes from kinesiology is strictly up to you. Co-creative living doesn't mean we're subservient to the energies and spirits of the earth. It's really an equal partnership.

Living co-creatively means that all on the earth is equal. In environmental sciences, it's known as an eco-system. Co-creative expands eco-system to include energies and spirit. This will include humans learning to "listen" (in whatever way we are able) to the spirits of the earth.

It requires protecting wild and natural senses of place.

It requires not dumping chemicals on crops, to get rid of a bug, which throws off the balance of nature.

Instead ...

We can feed the soil with compost and allow the healthy bugs to keep the balance of the plants. It allows for deer and moles to live with a garden. It allows for ancient stands of trees to be as they always have been – standing tall and being one with the earth ... undisturbed.

Energies and spirits of the earth see things we simply don't see – much as we see color and dogs don't – which is enormously helpful. But we have the physical ability to act, which they don't ... so they actually get fulfillment, as well.

Remember when I said that sensitivity training would later seem like pabulum?

The next book that John mentioned to us went even further ...

> *"Have you guys read the Kryon books?"*

Now we're going a little further out, but once your feet are in the water, and it seems odd but amazingly useful, why not see what the deeper water is like?

Kryon selected Lee Carroll to channel messages. Kryon is an entity that refers to itself as "Kryon, of Magnetic Service." In the mid 1980s, Kryon came here to adjust the magnetic grid around the world. (Scientists will tell you, by the way, that the grid had shifted, though they don't really know what caused it. It took Kryon several years to do, but the magnetic north pole is not where it used to be, so there is some of the verification I like.)

Lee records each channeling, and has it transcribed. He then combines several transcripts into a book of 200 or so pages. There are now eleven such books. I'm not a fast reader, and the reading was cumbersome for me – but – amazing! I'm not an idiot, but some the concepts weren't clear to me ... until Kryon gave illustrations and examples ... which did clarify the ideas.

The concepts are not the kind of things we think about normally. But ...

I can't think of ideas that are of any greater importance.

And do they relate to "sustainability"?

Without question ... yes!

Without finding the right spot in the right book, to quote passages, here's what I see – from memory – will be happening. It jibes perfectly with all of the visions cited in books such as *Apocalypse 2012*. And at this point, it does make sense. And – recalling my experience in market research, when I see multiple independent sources all pointing to the same trend, or conclusion, it does seem to happen.

There was a time in which we were definitely heading toward the end ... a burnt-out planet Earth and essentially the end of civilization. And ...

All the data I've been tracking for about twenty years actually supports that possibility, so it's no surprise. And many of the long-term historic forecasts saw the end of the millennium as the time of Armageddon and the end of the Earth. However, according to Kryon, there was a "shift" during the 1980s. It gave potential for a new era for mankind and civilization. 2012, a year that we thought might "live in infamy," now seems to be ...

The end of one major period of history and the beginning of another.

The new era will be fantastic – better than we can imagine.

But the *transition* from old to new will be painful.

Kryon describes the separation between non-physical entities and our physical world as a "veil." And the veil is thinning. The ease with which we'll be able to communicate with non-physical entities will be much greater, so co-creative living will likely be a cornerstone of our coming civilization.

Our past two thousand years has been dominated by male energy. If you recall the yin and yang model, yang tends to be competitive and features central authorities.

Are you familiar with the terms "zero-sum games" and "non-zero-sum games"?

In a zero-sum game, if I get ten points, you must lose ten points, so the sum remains zero. By definition, there must be a winner and a loser. All of our sports are built on that model. It's strategic, engaging, exciting, and very emotional ...

"The thrill of victory and the agony of defeat."

Now, let me share the problem we're facing in making the transition to a sustainable world. Here's a description of a little exercise I use in some workshops, to illustrate the same phenomenon ...

- Begin by forming two groups, the "AB" group and the "XY" group. Groups need to be in separate spaces, so they can confer privately.

- The exercise has multiple "rounds." For each round, the AB group selects an A or a B, and the XY group an X or a Y. The outcome of the selections has four possible combinations, with the outcome:

  An AX gives each group 3 points.
  An AY gives the XY group 6 points, and the AB group loses 6 points.
  A BX give the AB group 6 points, and the XY group loses 6 points.
  And a BY gives each group a loss of 3 points.

And to intensify the exercise ...

Some rounds are doubled or even squared – as some real-world situations are more vital than others. And there are opportunities for representatives of each team to meet, in a neutral space, and make agreements – except –that all agreements are made in good faith.

There's no "legal system" to enforce agreements.

Very quickly, you can see that the only way to "win" is to collaborate ... each team plays an AX. However, if my AB team plays an A, we're also very vulnerable. The essential ingredient in getting to AX is ...

Trust.

Even after representatives meet, teams can still sabotage one another. I've seen all sorts of strategies, counter strategies, and treachery. The drama can be strong!

Then, when the game ends and the groups come back together, the dialogue is thick. Suddenly, people realize, the game never really ends.

I've facilitated this little game scores of times. In only *one* instance did the two groups simply – and without much dialogue – make AX decisions. And they held to those decisions throughout every round. It was not dramatic. In fact, it was almost boring ... as there was no "contest." But – both teams got a lot of points.

Here's the bottom line:

> If you're in a zero-sum situation, then the yang competitive style is essential. There can be only one Super Bowl winner.

> If you're in a non-zero sum situation, then the yin collaborative style is essential. Everyone can win.

However – and this describes the predicament we're in today, globally ...

If you're in a non-zero-sum situation and you use the yang competitive style ... <u>everyone</u> ultimately loses!

If we think the world has only a limited amount of resources, we use the yang approach, so we can enjoy a good life.

> *"I want your oil (or your food or water.) And if I think there isn't enough for both of us, I'll attack you and take yours. There can be only one!"*

If we think the world actually has sufficient resources to provide food, clothing, power, and shelter for everyone – which it actually does, if managed properly – and if we still use the yang style, we then end up with the lose-lose outcome ...

If members of a family get competitive with one another, the whole family suffers, relationships deteriorate, and it could break up.

If the offense and defense of a football team blame one another for poor performance and mistakes, the whole team loses.

If two divisions in a company fight one another – for recognition, or bonuses, or any other rewards … the total company suffers.

And looking at what our civilization has been doing of late …

If we deplete natural resources – such as wiping out entire mountains in West Virginia – because it's cheaper to mine the coal that way, we make more money for a while – but we wipe out local communities, suffer law-suits, and eventually run out of coal. Lose-lose.

If we use native populations to get cheap labor, so we can grow tiger prawns less expensively, we engender hostility, destroy what had been good farmland, and eventually run out of places to farm.

Many studies have been done to see if Earth had sufficient renewable resources to support us. I cited Stanford's study of 8,000 sites in the world and found that using wind, alone, we could generate sufficient power for all mankind's uses – including accommodating growth. The same conclusions were reached regarding food.

Now let me shift back to the non-physical side of sustainability.

I think you can relate to the descriptions I gave of my Monroe Institute experiences. And you probably also read some of those unusual accounts of people not getting on a plane or entering a building because a voice told them not to do so. And I shared information about Findhorn and Perelandra – which show tangible evidence of the benefit of co-creative work. When Kryon says …

"The veil is thinning."

What exactly does that mean?

Throughout history, we've run across clairvoyants. The people around whom every religion has been formed were clairvoyants. If you go to the initial writings of any or all of them, the message is essentially the same. We also have instances such as Nostradamus, or Rudolph Steiner, or Edgar Cayce.

Nostradamus would get visions of future events or conditions and simply report them, almost as if he were taking dictation.

Steiner could give a talk to farmers on Monday – which might lead to biodynamic farming. Then, on Wednesday…

He'd speak to physicians – which might lead to homeopathic medicine. And he'd speak to educators on Friday – which might lead to the Waldorf Schools. How could he do that? He simply received guidance from the other side of the veil.

In co-creative living, when you pose a question, looking for help, it isn't always the same entity that provides the response. If it relates to your garden, it could be a garden deva. If it relates to the entire planet, it could be Gaia. Or, if it relates to you, it could be your higher self (i.e., ISH.)

(We're way past "sustainability" being "food, clothing and shelter" now!)

And if the "veil" – which seems to be the term entities use to describe the separation between their domain and ours – gets thinner, we could have more clairvoyants ... many more people who are able to receive messages directly from entities.

In England, when someone who's clairvoyant wishes to use his or her ability as a counselor or therapist, he or she has to be licensed, which is based on the person's ability to perform. (For example, a clairvoyant might be asked what ailment a person has. Then a physician does diagnostics, to see if the clairvoyant was correct.)

Earlier, I mentioned Lee Carroll. He channels for Kryon and has written about the "Indigo Children," people who can help us ease the transition to sustainable living.

Nancy Ann Tappe has an unusual trait – which might also be called an affliction. When she looks at people, she sees their color ... their "life color." (It's not a learned skill, it's just what she sees when she looks at people.) Several years ago, she suddenly stumbled on someone who gave off an indigo color – which she had never seen before. The indigos seem able to operate more comfortably on both sides of the veil, giving them special traits. From *"The Indigo Children"* ...

- They enter the world with a feeling of royalty and often act like it.

- They have a feeling of "deserving to be here," and are surprised when others don't share that.

- Self-worth is not a big issue.

- They have difficulty with absolute authority – authority without explanation or choice.

- They simply do not do certain things. For example, waiting in line is difficult for them.

- They get frustrated with systems that are ritual-oriented and don't require creative thought. In addition ...

They often see better ways of doing things, both at home and in school, which makes them seem like "systems breakers" – non-conforming to any system.

- They seem antisocial, unless they are with their own kind. If there are no others of like consciousness around them, they will often turn inward, feeling like no other human understands them. School is often very difficult for them socially.

- They will not respond to "guilt discipline." And ...

- They are not shy about letting you know what they need.

The indigos evidently began appearing in the '80s. Many of these observations and conclusions were done while they were in grade school. Then, another book was done ten years later, as the indigos matured and entered the work force. Some observations from *"The Indigo Children Ten Years Later"* ...

- Indigo kids are much better at home study, rather than being in the traditional school setting.

- They'll change the world. By 2018, we'll live in a world that is very different than the one in which we grew up.

- For indigos, respect fosters respect ... which creates a communication style that's more interpersonally successful and satisfying.

- The majority of indigos just know that there's something important for them to do in this world. *"They have knowingness about being here. They're eager to explore different ways of thinking, even if they've claimed a particular point of view, religion or mode of thought."*

- Indigos feel a connection to a higher power and consciousness. It's part of their interdimensional wiring.

- Indigos embrace emotion as an all-encompassing aspect of communications. Their communication is interdimensional and emotion inclusive. They share feelings as naturally as they breathe.

- Indigos want their generation to contribute their vision, skills, and intellect to create new thinking in the global marketplace regarding diversity, values, ethics, technology, and purpose.

Now, how will government, education, the economy, business management, and even families appear under the influence of indigo leadership?

Indigos will be positive, optimistic, and even passionate ... although there will be challenges, conflicts, and suffering to overcome in order to build a new society. The indigos are coming to accelerate destruction of walls that separate the old from the new energy, thus clearing the way for the expression of consciousness, evolution, and freedom of being. (That's why they're so important to sustainability.)

Indigo leadership is spontaneous and charismatic. Their way of being in the world delights people. Their traits include: humility, cooperativeness, solidarity, integrity, spirituality, sensitivity, and the facility to create a consensus about higher values. They have a capacity to foresee the future and to capture those visions.

These leaders of the future will have vision, and be guided by ...

Intuition.

I can go on, to describe other traits of indigos. But what I've learned is that, as we're nearing the close of a major chapter in human civilization, they are born with different "wiring" that enables them to get guidance more easily from the other side of the veil, to create positive visions, and provide leadership...in the yin style.

I shared my history with you, and you know that I'm not psychic – or indigo. But I do exist here on Earth, as you do. I have a reasonable brain, and I have energy to do things that I think are important. I also have experienced the benefits of living co-creatively ... which is why I believe that's what's coming will be magnificent.

What I have learned so far about working with entities is ...

- They beat Google all to pieces! You can ask absolutely anything at all and get really good answers ... and not just data, but wise counsel. You can also ask why they suggest something, and they explain, in whatever detail you wish, without ever getting defensive.

- If you don't follow their advice – because it's our responsibility to act – they never chastise or guilt you, or say, *"I told you so."*

- And their sole goal is to be helpful ... as absolutely helpful as possible. Their goal is for us to lead rich, fulfilling lives ... especially as our goals also contribute to the fulfillment of all mankind, and to the enrichment of all plants, minerals, and animals on our Earth.

And – the guidance is free; you have absolutely no obligations.

When's the last time you had a partner like that?

Now, how does a non-indigo person like me go about doing all this?

1. Kinesiology. While structuring everything in yes/no format can be tedious, if you have the patience, you can get the counsel.

2. Intuition. I think we've all had times when we get a "hunch" or a "notion" about something. It's not an emotion, and it certainly isn't as concrete as written or verbal messages. Intuition usually comes from your higher self, (ISH,) but it can come from any entity. The problem I have is: trusting it. Am I doing wishful thinking, or is it true guidance? It's a subtle communication medium, and I'm better with concrete things.

Well, you can see that my journey into sustainability went way beyond "saving 30% on my utility bills." And even beyond the measurable physical domain.

What's next?

Circa 2009: The Journey to Come

As I sit here, looking out at the future, I begin to think about where our world will be heading in the next few years, and what the most prudent set of actions for me to take will be. I'll begin by reflecting on a few articles ...

Futurist John Petersen responded to an e-mail from a friend of his who saw the fear index at its lowest levels in long while, and thought that maybe the problem was past. John didn't agree ...

"First of all, the financial issues are systemic – they are a product of the structure of the system and they are intrinsically not sustainable. The system will continue going until it crashes. The crash is inevitable; it is just unknown exactly when it is going to happen. This is no different conceptually than knowing that if you overdraw your checking account, at some point the bank is going to bounce your checks. It's that predictable. The indicators abound.

"But the bigger, far more interesting question is whether this confluence of very visible events is part of some larger, much more profound change that will not return us to the status quo ante. This is not some arcane, academic type of question. There are a large number of compelling indicators that suggest that this is the case.

"Elliot Wave theorists say that there is an extraordinary confluence of historical waves showing up now that presages huge change. Assessments of historical cycles of 'novelty' predict big shifts are coming. Many indigenous prophets and shamans say the big change that has been prophesied for centuries is now upon us. And then, if you want to really reach out in unconventional space, there are many psychics and channels who point to October (2009) or some time later (but soon) for a very significant disruption.

"Why even mention these psychics and channels? Well, we are living in a time of unprecedented, exponential change. There is no question about this in terms of population growth, species depletion, science discoveries, natural resource usage, technological innovation, and information and knowledge growth. The size and metabolism of the system in which we live is getting far larger and more complex at such extraordinary rates that it is now beyond human ability to understand it.

"We need to be looking at every source and capability we can find that might give us a fix on what might be on our horizon. We also know from former highly classified programs that some of the intuitives have generated very extraordinary and accurate intelligence for the U.S. and Soviet governments in the past. It works. What do these sources say?

"They're pretty universal in describing an epochal shift that could be described as nothing less than the largest punctuation in evolution that our species has ever experienced – extraordinary change in a short period of time. The issue at hand is:

"How do you alert people to a looming potentiality that is so large that no one alive has any reasonable means of visualizing it?

"How do you get people to begin to consider something that could be essentially unfathomable in any conventional terms?"

So, here I sit in late 2009, sensing that some enormous changes are about to happen, and wondering exactly what I need to do to prepare for them, and to whom I can turn for help. Here's a great example of what people might be able to do, if government can provide support or, at least, not get in the way ...

Dr. Michael Hamm is the C. S. Mott Professor of Sustainable Agriculture, at Michigan State University. He focuses on ways to provide access to healthy, locally grown food. So ...

- I've already cited the coming food shortage, and that doesn't even take population growth and erosion of arable land into account.

- Many of the "Rust Belt" cities – where the economy is the worst – have a large number of totally abandoned houses. In Flint, Michigan, 40% of the houses are abandoned.

- The county has land-banked 1,100 derelict houses that were repossessed by Flint for failure to pay taxes ... 800 acres of lots.

Dr. Hamm and his students began working with the county to change things ...

- The county initiated a "clean and green" program in which 1,100 houses were removed. The city also owns 4,800 more parcels and expects to add 2,000 more in a matter of months.

- Dr. Hamm and his students plan to us some of these inner-city plots to put up "hoop houses" (inexpensive greenhouses,) grow crops, set up farmers' markets, and sell produce for local school lunches.

- With 700 acres in production, Dr. Hamm estimates satisfying half of all Flint's produce needs, providing local employment, and eliminating transportation costs (for people and produce.)

Then the hitch surfaced ...

City ordinances prohibit such activities. And, there's resistance to selling residential lots to farmers, in case, at some point, the city begins to repopulate. They're not sure whether to hold onto that land, to hold open the possibility for growth, or to feed and care for the people who already live there.

The project is at a standstill.

I ran into the same problem when we implemented rainwater harvesting. Our Garden Atrium homes each have a cistern that satisfies all the non-potable needs of residents – essentially toilets and hose bibs. But that's 95% of our home's water use. Instead of paying $90 every three months, we pay only $3 or so. And – with the region beginning to run short of water, it contributes to overall sustainability. But the city regulators raised objections ...

- First, they said that our water would have to be pre-treated before it could be discharged into the sewer system.

- And second, they said that rainwater cannot be discharged into the sanitary sewer system.

Well, the reason for the first regulation is for industries that have toxic discharges that can't be handled by a normal wastewater treatment plant; it's not intended for residential use. And the second regulation is intended to prevent masses of rainwater overloading the sanitary sewer system. Now, the Garden Atriums have no toxic discharge. And the volume of wastewater each home sends to the sewer system is no different than a home sending city-treated water to the system.

So, even though we were being more sustainable and equally healthful, we encountered sufficient resistance that we had to call in our attorneys.

In looking at all the trends, I doubt that the governing systems that got us into this bind will be the systems that can get us out of the bind. That lack of confidence is reflected in the Gallup survey. The solution will need to come from ...

Me.

And from you. And ...

From individuals ... at "grassroots" levels.

My thinking has really evolved over the course of this journey. I began with how to save money on power consumption with more efficient light bulbs, and I ended with living co-creatively. That's an enormous shift. At one point, I wondered ...

> "What is the _ultimate_ goal for all of this effort?"

"Am I here to just enjoy a good life for my family and myself?"

"Am I here to see how much I can learn and grow?"

"Am I here to accomplish certain things?"

I think we all ponder these questions from time to time. So, I asked the questions (co-creatively,) and quickly got a one-word intuitive sense ...

Oneness!

Then I used kinesiology to verify my intuition and got a "yes."

Everything is connected to everything.

We are *one* with animals, plants, and the earth.

And each of us has goals for our life – though I hadn't always overtly thought about what they were and how I'd accomplish them.

My personal long-term goal, then, will be to get clearer about what would be most fulfilling for me. And I can use co-creative methods to help me do that. Without a long-term goal, a "path," I'll have no idea what my best "first step" should be.

Right now, I believe my long-term goal will be to create a totally sustainable community – the village described previously – and use that community as a model. Learn, from living experience, what needs to be added or deleted or adjusted to make the community an amazing life experience for all its residents. And I'd want to use the community as a model from which others can learn. It's a classroom.

I believe our future world will comprise a large number of small communities, such as the sustainable village I envision ... a network that allows us to ...

"Live local, but think global."

As to the first ten steps I might have to take to get there, I recall the comments of John Petersen, earlier in this chapter ...

"How do you alert people to a looming potentiality that is so large that no one alive has any reasonable means of visualizing it?

"How do you get people to begin to consider something that could be essentially unfathomable in any conventional terms?"

Personally, I try to visualize what might "get broken" so that I can take steps to address it *now* ... kind of like preventive medicine. So, for example ...

- We keep a supply of cash in the house, in case our government declares a "bank holiday" – which did happen recently in England.

- As the dollar is likely to plummet in value, for the many reasons previously cited, we bought a few ounces of gold.

- If food shortages hit, which seems likely, we are buying large quantities of items that do not deteriorate. Unit price is less, too. We also have developed a dialogue with a local farmer who produces organic produce, and a seafood supplier who buys from the watermen.

If the trends that seem imminent never do happen, we've really lost nothing. So perhaps the biggest suggestion I can offer is to do some *"What if?"* thinking. Then, we're not only better prepared, but if those events do transpire, we won't be as shocked and we won't suffer from the "deer in the headlights" syndrome.

If this book helps you do that, and helps you through the transition I believe is coming ... and then helps you to enjoy a more joyous quality of life than you've had before ... I'd consider this effort to be worthwhile.

The responsibility – for ourselves and for our earth – lies with *each* of us.

In thinking about creating a truly sustainable environment, at one with all of nature and in which we can all enjoy as absolutely fulfilling a life experience as possible, I thought about Nicholas Cage's comment in the film, *"National Treasure,"* citing our Declaration of Independence ...

> *"It is our right, it is our duty, to envision and to create an environment that enables us to enjoy life, liberty, and the pursuit of happiness."*

The responsibility – for ourselves and for our earth – lies with *each* of us. It's time to leave our campsite better than it was when we got here!

It's time for each of us to ask ourselves ...

"What, specifically, can I <u>do</u> that will make a positive difference?"

I've come to believe that living sustainably needs to be even <u>more</u> than ...

> Living with the earth, or living co-creatively.
> Being grateful for what we have.
> Or even honoring who we are.

I think back to that section of my research that dealt with happiness and quality of life, without which, we're just surviving. So I'll finish with a quote from D ...

"When one is filled with joy, one does not feel the need to hurt, abuse, or harm anyone or anything – including oneself.

"When one feels joy, one has no need to buy things to fill a void.

"When one feels joy, one has no need to dominate.

"When one feels joy, one feels the need to protect and help others. And one helps others from a healthy place, so it remains joyful to the person doing the giving.

"When one feels joy, one feels a need to live more simply.

"When one feels joy, one feels a need to protect Mother Earth and all her creatures.

"When one feels joy, one chooses to live in balance.

"We are all mirrors of our inner world. People will see someone who is joyous and will want to know ...

"How did you become that way?"

Think about those moments in your life that you would call "peak positive experiences" ... your wedding ... your graduation ... the birth of your child ... some major award or recognition. Those are true "moments of joy" in our lives. Now think about similar experiences you've had that are not related to human events ...

- A magnificent sunset.
- A spectacular view from a mountaintop.
- The serenity of a frozen lake covered with a fresh snowfall.

Now think of enjoying those kinds of feelings each and every day. *That* is the goal of sustainable living, not saving 30% on your utility bill. You've now read about – and seen – how you can live quite elegantly with what comes to your home site, naturally ... with few or no utility bills. But – if we live that way and still don't enjoy lives that are totally fulfilling – for each of us – we're surviving, not sustaining.

At the start of this book, I said that my purpose was to share a picture with you of what has a high potential of occurring ... and soon. And even more important, I think what's in store for us – despite the inevitable trauma of transition – will be ...

FANTASTIC!

As you've now seen, this *is* much more than wishful thinking. There *will* be wonderful "light" at the other end of this tunnel. We're going through a transition to a whole new era in the evolution of mankind. And that, truly, is "Sustainability."

Stuart W. Rose, Ph.D., earned his doctorate in Organization Development, has been a professor at three major universities, and has worked for several decades as an educator and a consultant to architects, consulting engineers, and other design professionals. He is a registered architect, as well as a graduate structural engineer. For nearly twenty years he has tracked trends related to the ability to sustain life on Earth and has initiated a unique pilot project of sustainable housing. His *Garden Atriums* project has been featured in nearly two dozen local, regional, and national newspapers and magazines, on NPR, PBS, and on major regional television programs. Rose has presented his work and his expertise at three international sustainability conferences.

Made in the USA
Charleston, SC
21 August 2011